For Kian,

Blessings!

Your friend,

Ray

GOD AND POLITICS

HOW CAN A CHRISTIAN BE IN POLITICS?

★ ROY HERRON ★

Library of Congress Cataloging-in-Publication Data

Herron, Roy.

   God and politics/ Roy Herron ; Daniel Taylor, general editor.

      p.cm.

   Includes bibliographical references and index.

   ISBN-13: 978-1-4143-2305-3 (sc)

   ISBN-10: 1-4143-2305-0 (sc)

1. Christianity and politics—United States. I. Taylor, Daniel, date. II. Title.

BR526.H43 2008

261.70973—dc22   2008005591

Printed in the United States of America

14	13	12	11	10	09	08
7	6	5	4	3		

For my beloved sister, Betsye,
who married outside the party
but always kept the faith.
Your courageous laughter in the face of cancer
bears strong witness to the Lord of life.

★

CONTENTS

★

CONTENTS

INTRODUCTION

★

"What are you working on?" my son John asked when he came into our home library before going to school.

"A book on faith and politics," I replied.

John quickly and skeptically asked, *"Do they go together?"*

John speaks for most people.

This is about two topics one should never raise in polite conversation: religion and politics. Ms. Manners would caution us not to mention either, much less both at once. But in America, religion and politics were siblings before the states were united. The founders drew on religious ideals and rhetoric as they created our republic.

In 1775, John Adams wrote his wife, Abigail, "Statesmen may plan and speculate for Liberty, but it is Religion and Morality alone which can establish the principles upon which Freedom can securely stand." Adams believed that "a patriot must be a religious man."[1]

The original draft of the Declaration of Independence referred to the "laws of nature and of nature's God" and the "Creator" who endows us with "certain inalienable rights."[2] The Second Continental Congress inserted into Thomas Jefferson's document two more references to God, appealing "to the supreme judge of the world" and referring to delegates' "firm reliance on the protection of divine providence."[3]

When the Constitutional Convention struggled in a fierce debate in 1787, Benjamin Franklin emphasized the importance of religion for America's past, present, and future: "I have lived, Sir, a long time, and the longer I live, the more convincing proofs I see of this truth—that God governs in the affairs of men. And if a sparrow cannot fall to the ground without His notice, is it probable that an empire can rise without His aid? We have been assured, Sir, in the Sacred Writings, that 'except the Lord build the House, they labor in vain that build it.' I firmly believe this; and I also believe that without His concurring aid we shall succeed in this political building no better than the Builders of Babel."[4]

When our nation's first president gave his farewell address, George Washington warned, "Of all the dispositions and habits, which lead to political prosperity, Religion and morality are indispensable supports...Reason and experience both forbid us to expect that national morality can prevail in exclusion of a religious principle."[5]

In that tradition, this book seeks to explore, using both ancient Scripture and contemporary experience, how a Christian can be in politics today. Accordingly, I write as a confessing Christian and a practicing politician.

I grew up in a home where asking a blessing before meals and saying prayers before bed were daily facts of life. A caring, loving church family nurtured me. In college I learned from and worshipped with fired-up friends at a Baptist student union, excited evangelicals in an interdenominational group, and faithful Methodists and Roman Catholics at an interfaith center. I studied New Testament and ethics in Scotland before returning to the States for a joint program in divinity and law. I worked in campus ministry, preached at local churches, and served in small ways from the rural South to New York City's Hell's Kitchen. Then I returned to my hometown where I practiced law to support my preaching habit. As our church's full-time minister observed, "We pay Roy a dollar a year, and it only takes three sermons to get our money's worth."

Finally I fell from the pulpit to the pit of politics. In defense, I offer two mitigating circumstances: a rough family and a tough neighborhood.

My family included county legislators, sheriffs, a state legislator, a judge, and a federal law enforcement agent. Within two blocks of our home during my mother's lifetime have resided five mayors, five legislators, four or five judges, a public service commissioner, and the Speaker of the state House of Representatives who later became governor. Frequently visiting relatives on our block were two U.S. senators, including one who became vice president.

Such family members and neighbors bore witness that public service could be an honest, even honorable, way to love your neighbor as yourself.

In high school and college, I worked for my U.S. congressman and the Speaker of the Tennessee House of Representatives. After law and divinity school, I worked with members of the U.S. House of Representatives and the Senate and in a presidential campaign. When my state representative became governor, I ran for his seat. I now have served almost two decades in the Tennessee House and Senate.

I write this book for Christians, though I hope others also will find it useful. I do not intend to exclude, and I surely do not wish to demean, other faiths or their faithful. I do, however, write—and serve—out of my own faith, and I pray my experiences will be useful to other Christians confronting questions about politics and public service.

My shortcomings notwithstanding, God knows we need Christians in politics. We need politics to be practiced faithfully. In sum and substance, we need *faithful politics*.

CHAPTER 1

HOW CAN A CHRISTIAN BE IN POLITICS?

*Politics: The art of looking for trouble, finding it
everywhere, diagnosing it wrongly, and applying
unsuitable remedies.*
ERNEST BENN

Politics is a beautiful word to me!
SENATOR ANNA BELLE CLEMENT O'BRIEN

*He who refuses to rule is liable to be ruled by one who is
worse than himself.*
PLATO

"**H**ow can you be a *Christian* and be in *politics?*" I hear this
question from people of faith all the time. They seem
startled that a former minister has run for and serves in public office.

I recall once when I was about to preach at a church near Nashville.
Johnny Hayes, a member of that congregation, introduced me by
telling of a political fundraiser he had attended the night before that
honored a one-hundred-year-old gentleman. Johnny asked the
centenarian how he had survived so long and so well as a member of
a small minority in a county dominated by the other political party.
The gentleman's sage reply was, "Johnny, you've just got to know
who you can trust and who you can't trust."

When Johnny asked just whom one can and cannot trust, the old man allegedly replied, "There are just three types of folks you can't trust. You can't trust lawyers, you can't trust preachers, and you can't trust politicians."

Johnny turned to me sitting behind the pulpit, squirming on the overstuffed chair, and said, "This fellow here is a lawyer, a preacher, and last week he went to work in a political campaign—you can't believe a *thing* he says!"

The congregation roared with laughter.

It was not the first time that I'd been the victim of a good joke. After all, I am a lawyer. But even lawyers are more respected than politicians.

I will never forget the letter a student wrote me not long after I began serving in the legislature. I'd represented her parents as an attorney a few years earlier.

> Dear Mr. Herron,
>
> My name is Candy and my Mom and Dad think a lot of you since your days with Legal Aid so I chose to write you as part of a school assignment. What I'd like to know is, what inspired you to move from the Legal Aid Office (where you were a big help to the people) to being a state representative?

Implicit in Candy's question was doubt, even at a young age, that one could do good in politics.

How should we answer Candy's question? Can a Christian do good in politics?

WHAT IS POLITICS?

To answer Candy's question and many others, we can begin by asking what the word *politics* means. We get the word, as well as some of our central ideas about politics, from the ancient Greeks. For them, the term *politics* referred to the interactions of Greek citizens in their city-state, the *polis*. As one scholar puts it, "Politics is the polis, or civil community, ordering its life together on the basis of the public good. And to be human is to be a participant in that kind of community."[1] In fact, the Greeks considered any person outside the polis to be a nonhuman, a "barbarian."[2]

All the terms in this definition are important as we think about politics: *civil, community, ordering, life together, public good*. The common denominator is the concept of organizing our shared experience. Politics involves what we do together to try to make our shared life better, recognizing that sometimes the actual result can be that we make our lives together worse.

The organized face of politics is government. Government is the collection of institutions and laws that develop out of the often-messy process of people engaged in politics. We may like or dislike our particular government, but it is what we have made ourselves in our attempt to create a better life together. If we more or less like the government we have, we ought to maintain it and keep it healthy. If we don't like the government we have, we should change it for the better. In both cases we will be involved in politics.

In this book, then, I use the term *politics* to describe the American process of electing our leaders and the process of their serving us. Generally, I use the term in a neutral, descriptive way. But not *everyone* is so inclined.

A NEGATIVE VIEW OF POLITICS

Many of us feel we have all the government we can stand and more than we can afford. We strongly, instinctively react against politics when we consider waste, fraud, corruption, deception, arrogance, misuse of authority, and burdensome taxes. Many people of faith hold this view of politics and government, and they also believe that government in recent decades has contributed to moral decline and the weakening of traditional values.

Anger and frustration toward government today are very high. But if you find yourself frustrated with government, imagine how frustrated we elected officials feel when we try to make government work and often cannot. Time and again, my task is not, as I would wish, to pass needed laws or set up helpful programs, but rather to try to stop bad bills and simply make existing laws and programs work. Often I work to get government to help people, but perhaps even more often I try to keep it from hindering or even harming citizens.

Like my father before me, I get edgy around April 15 when my wife and I calculate our federal taxes. I've seen governments waste money much too often. I've even known corrupt people in government who stole public funds. I know too well how fallen our government and its officials can be.

A POSITIVE VIEW OF POLITICS

As frustrating and maddening as government and politics can be, they are necessary, and they are often forces for good.

I served in the Tennessee General Assembly with a wonderful senator named Anna Belle Clement O'Brien. Senator O'Brien started hundreds of talks and speeches with these words: "Politics is a beautiful word to me!"

She would explain, "Politics is how crippled children walk, the mentally ill get care, roads are built, health care is provided, children are taught."

It is through the political process, through electing people to represent us, that government works, doing the things we ourselves—as the *polis*—ask it to do.

Among other things, we ask governments to provide for the national defense; build roads, airports, courthouses, and jails; foster a business climate for economic prosperity;

> It is through the political process that government works.

protect workers; support needy children; protect us from hazardous wastes and deadly poisons; educate our children; prevent and punish crime; promote good health and prevent epidemics; and defend our constitutional rights to free speech, association, and worship.

Indeed, whether we respect our governments or not, we ask them to play important and positive roles in the life of every American citizen. I submit that, for all the flaws, our American political system is a blessing that too often we take for granted. And no one owes government more than I do. Here is why.

HOW POLITICS SAVED MY CHILDREN

About nine weeks into my wife's first pregnancy, we went for the initial ultrasound. The doctor moved the wand around in what I told my wife was the same purple grease I used on our tractor and equipment when I was a boy working on my family's farm. After a few moments, the doctor said, "See the little heartbeat?"

We did see sort of a pulsation—the heartbeat of our firstborn-to-be.

"And look, there's a second heartbeat," the doctor stated rather calmly. "Twins."

I started laughing as Nancy gasped for breath.

The doctor kept moving the wand around in the ultrasound jelly. I thought the doctor had done enough damage for one day and started to ask her to stop, but I waited too long. Suddenly the doctor sounded excited: "What's *that* over there? Are there *three*?"

A few minutes later, the doctor finally announced, "I think there are *just two* babies."

I never thought I would be relieved to be having "just two babies." Of course, I had never even conceived, so to speak, of having twins. Of all the things I thought might befall me, this simply was not one.

Still, we left the office thankful that we were having "just two" babies. Stunned, but relieved there were not *three*.

A DOCTOR RECOMMENDS ABORTION

Ten weeks later we received another jolt. Our doctors discovered complications in the pregnancy. A specialist in high-resolution ultrasound told us there were two little boys, probably identical. I immediately teased my wife, because she had grown up with her mother, her

> We left the office thankful that we were having "just two" babies.

grandmother, her sister, a female dog, and her five-to-one outnumbered father. I told Nancy that to achieve true gender justice, I would go get a male, bird-dog puppy.

As the exam went on, we joked about possible names. I modestly suggested Roy Jr. and Roy III. She quickly rejected that idea. We laughed out loud, and it truly was one of the happiest moments of our lives. Meanwhile, the doctor continued his work.

Then the specialist told us the twins had a condition that he had seen only sixteen times. In fifteen of those sixteen cases, both twins had died. The sixteenth time, one of the twins died.

Thirty-two babies. Thirty-one dead.

He told us our twins were not going to live. He recommended an abortion.

"How sure are you, Doctor?" I asked.

The doctor said he was pretty sure.

"Like 90, 95, 98 percent certain?"

He replied with a single word: "Yes."

The doctor again recommended an abortion.

In twenty-four hours, we had six consultations with three doctors at two hospitals.

Further tests and a visit with a high-risk pregnancy specialist named Sal Lombardi led to a more hopeful prognosis. If Nancy could carry the boys several more weeks, Dr. Lombardi told us we *might* yet take two boys home.

BIRTH DAY

Nancy was the minister of discipleship at a church in Nashville, but the congregation—and many other friends—ministered to her during that time. Her Bible study group met in our little apartment as Nancy went on "modified bed rest." We saw Dr. Lombardi weekly during much of the summer, and finally in late July, he told us to come in daily. Standard protocol at that time had only required visits every third day, but just the week before a couple with triplets had experienced the death of one of their babies, so he changed the protocol with us.

Dr. Lombardi was trying to delay the delivery as long as possible so that the larger baby, whose lungs were not yet fully developed, could have a better chance of surviving. But he did not want to wait so long that the supply of blood to the smaller baby diminished so much that it killed him.

He literally was trying to balance the life of one twin against the other.

Seven weeks before the due date, on August 2, primary election day, we were told, "You can go to the hospital. You're going to deliver today." While the larger baby's lungs still were not as developed as Dr. Lombardi wanted, to wait any longer would endanger the

Though a doctor recommended an abortion, the Herrons chose life. Both twins survived and now attend college.

smaller baby. In fact, he said if we waited even a single day longer, the smaller baby would probably die.

John and Rick were born that day. That marked the end of one difficult period and the beginning of another. Living in a neonatal intensive care unit for twenty-eight days straight was more than we ever wanted. But we were so thankful our sons were alive. After four weeks, they sent us home from the hospital with both boys.

THE POLITICS OF LIFE AND DEATH

So, what does this story have to do with you and with politics?

Dr. Sal Lombardi, the high-risk pregnancy specialist who decided that our twins' birthday would not be their death day, graduated from public schools, then went to college and medical school on federally subsidized student loans. He developed his extraordinary expertise by learning from taxpayer-funded teachers in government-funded universities and hospitals.

Dr. Doug Brown, the obstetrician who so skillfully delivered our babies and took care of Nancy, received government-subsidized education and training.

The neonatologists who kept our babies alive also received government-funded education and training, as did many of the nurses whose care was essential for the boys' survival.

The hospital where our boys spent their first four weeks is part of a private university, but it receives literally millions and millions of tax dollars from our government.

But this is only part of how our boys were saved by government and tax dollars.

One of our premature babies was treated with *surfactant*, which helped his lungs develop so he could breathe and survive. That miracle-working, lifesaving drug was developed with millions of tax dollars made available through our federal government.

The neonatal intensive care unit (NICU) where our sons spent their first four weeks was itself an invention made possible and developed with both federal tax dollars and private donations.

Several other treatment techniques, procedures, and medicines that helped save our babies and literally thousands and thousands of others were developed with government funding.

Simply put, if not for the wise and compassionate decisions of men and women in government and the tax dollars paid by us all, my sons would have died. You can see, then, why I am unlikely to agree with any oversimplified depiction of

> Several other treatment techniques that helped save our babies were developed with government funding.

government as evil.

In America, politics selects and controls the governments that save lives—or don't. In America, politics and government are often forces for good. If sometimes they do not do their job as well as they should, then we should participate in the process and make them better.

Plato wrote, "He who refuses to rule is liable to be ruled by one who is worse than himself."[3]

And so it is for faithful Christians today. If people of faith refuse to participate in politics, then others will make the crucial decisions. In a democracy, the people get the government they choose—and work for. You could say we get the government we deserve.

Government can be awful, or it can be good; often it is some of both. It is our duty, both as citizens and as Christians, to make it better. The question, then, is not, how can a Christian be in politics? The question is, how can a Christian *not* be in politics?

CHAPTER 2

WHAT DOES THE BIBLE SAY?

*Seek the welfare of the city where I have sent you into exile,
and pray to the Lord on its behalf, for in its welfare you
will find your welfare.*
JEREMIAH 29:7

*The king will answer them, "Truly I tell you, just as you
did it to one of the least of these who are members of my
family, you did it to me."*
MATTHEW 25:40

*The mystery of the poor is this: That they are Jesus, and
what you do for them you do for Him.*
DOROTHY DAY

D oes the Bible tell us how to vote? No—and yes. No, the Bible
does not tell us specifically which candidate to vote for or what
party to support or what position to take on every issue. It does not
give a blanket endorsement of any political party, political system, or
political philosophy. In fact, it is likely to judge all these and find
them wanting because of their human limitations and fallenness.

At the same time, the Bible *does* give us guidance for voting and
conducting ourselves in the political arena as people of faith. It does
so by offering guidelines and principles—and specific historical
examples—that we can apply to present-day situations. Not
everyone will apply these biblical guidelines and principles the same

way or come to identical conclusions—or vote the same! But it is a great gift to us that we have this rich source of biblical wisdom to draw on, and we should commit ourselves to understanding and applying it as faithfully as we can.

The first epigraph at the beginning of this chapter captures the essence of a biblical understanding of citizenship and government: "Seek the welfare of the city ... for in its welfare you will find your welfare." This verse tells us many things, including that people of faith have an obligation to be good citizens and contribute to the welfare of their society. It suggests that in working for the good of others, we also work for our own good. To use a biblical term, we are contributing to and benefiting from *shalom*.

Most people associate the word *shalom* with peace, and that is certainly one of its primary meanings. But it refers to a peace that comes about when everything in a society is as it should be. *Shalom* describes the state of order and justice and righteousness that God intends for creation.

In the Old Testament, *shalom* is the state of wholeness that can include "health, prosperity, security, or the spiritual completeness of covenant."[1] It is "a wholesomeness determined and given by God."[2]

The New Testament equivalent of *shalom* is *eirene*, which usually is translated as "peace." Peace in the New Testament sometimes refers to the absence of war or strife, as in Luke 14:32 and Acts 12:20 (NIV). Peace is also used, however, to describe a restored relationship with God, as in Ephesians 2:14-22 and Colossians 1:20.[3] This "peaceful" relationship with God is also what God wants for human relationships in society. In fact, the Kingdom of God that Christ announces is the kingdom of *shalom*—everyone and everything in its place, and all relationships, human and divine, as God intends.

> *Shalom* describes the state of order and justice and righteousness that God intends for creation.

Perhaps the most famous reference to peace in the New Testament is the beatitude of Matthew 5:9, "Blessed are the peacemakers." These peacemakers are those "who create peace where there is hatred, who reconcile where there is separation."[4]

The highest purpose of politics is to achieve or repair that state of wholeness, fairness, and order that the word *shalom* describes. It will never be perfectly achieved in this life, but it is the ideal for which persons of faith are required to work.

Politics today seems to be the opposite of peacemaking. Political activity is increasingly marked by anger, unprincipled attacks, and mean-spiritedness. Political campaigns—and even everyday governance—are seen as wars. The Clinton–Gore presidential campaigns called their command center The War Room. Republican operative Lee Atwater relied on Sun Tzu's *The Art of War* for political strategy.

> The highest purpose of politics is to achieve or repair that state of wholeness, fairness, and order that the word *shalom* describes.

Closer to home, friends joke when they see me about to leave the district for the Capitol. "Off to the legislative wars again?" they ask—and too often they are not far off.

The ugliest campaign attacks I've endured came when a fellow Christian ran against me. His party's political operatives and some supporters spent many resources not promoting him but attacking my values and character. And this was a campaign between fellow believers.

SERVANT LEADERSHIP

The fight for political power and status is an old problem, not a modern political invention. Though the Bible is hardly a political primer, it speaks firmly to the powerful about the very nature of power and position. Remember the Gospel story of the disciples arguing about who was the greatest? You can almost hear them jockeying for a political position as Jesus' chief of staff, his top-gun disciple, his right-hand man. Here's how Mark tells it:

> Then they came to Capernaum; and when he was in the house he asked them, "What were you arguing

about on the way?" But they were silent, for on the way they had argued with one another who was the greatest. He sat down, called the twelve, and said to them, "Whoever wants to be first must be last of all and servant of all." Then he took a little child and put it among them; and taking it in his arms, he said to them, "Whoever welcomes one such child in my name welcomes me, and whoever welcomes me welcomes not me but the one who sent me."

MARK 9:33-37

How disheartening this must have been to Jesus. After all this time with his disciples, day in and day out, how little they have understood his message and his mission. So he sits down to teach them about greatness and power in the eyes of God. He starts with a rather nonsensical saying: "Whoever wants to be first must be last of all and servant of all."

Not certain this has cleared things up, Jesus provides a visual aid. He takes a child in his arms and explains, "Whoever welcomes one such child in my name welcomes me." In Jesus' day, to welcome someone meant to take them into one's home, to include them as part of one's family. To feed, clothe, and nurture them. All the things we do for our own children.

But the command to welcome the child, as Jesus describes it here, goes far beyond caring for our own little ones. In the time Jesus lived, children were utterly without status. They were considered "non-person[s]," "inconsequential," and "socially invisible."[5] And yet Jesus teaches that these inconsequential children are to be received as if they are Jesus himself, received "in [his] name."[6]

You might say that Jesus' idea of power and greatness is kind of like being foster parents who take in children no one else wants, who see their suffering when no one else does.

This same message of servant leadership is found throughout the New Testament. In Luke's account of the Last Supper, the disciples again get into a fight about who among them is the greatest. Jesus admonishes them:

> The kings of the Gentiles lord it over them; and those in authority over them are called benefactors. But not so with you; rather the greatest among you must become like the youngest, and the leader like one who serves. For who is greater, the one who is at the table or the one who serves? Is it not the one at the table? But I am among you as one who serves.
>
> LUKE 22:25-27

Paul understood and taught this. In Philippians 2:5-7, we find these words: "Let the same mind be in you that was in Christ Jesus, who, though he was in the form of God, did not regard equality with God as something to be exploited, but emptied himself, taking the form of a slave, being born in human likeness."

THE JUDGMENT OF THE NATIONS

If leaders are to be servants, where shall these servant leaders lead? What shall their nations be about?

The following Gospel passage is known as the Judgment of the Nations. Jesus tells us how nations will be judged—and how you and I will be judged.

> When the Son of Man comes in his glory, and all the angels with him, then he will sit on the throne of his glory. All the nations will be gathered before him, and he will separate people one from another as a shepherd separates the sheep from the goats, and he will put the sheep at his right hand and the goats at the left. Then the king will say to those at his right hand, "Come, you that are blessed by my Father, inherit the kingdom prepared for you from the foundation of the world; for I was hungry and you gave me food, I was thirsty and you gave me something to drink, I was a stranger and you welcomed me, I was naked and you gave me clothing, I was sick and you took care of me, I was in prison and you visited me." Then the righteous will answer him, "Lord, when was it that we saw you hungry and gave you food, or thirsty and gave you something to drink? And when was it that we saw you a stranger and welcomed you, or naked and gave you clothing? And when was it that we saw you sick or in prison and visited you?" And the king will answer them,

"Truly I tell you, just as you did it to one of the least of these who are members of my family, you did it to me." Then he will say to those at his left hand, "You that are accursed, depart from me into the eternal fire prepared for the devil and his angels; for I was hungry and you gave me no food, I was thirsty and you gave me nothing to drink, I was a stranger and you did not welcome me, naked and you did not give me clothing, sick and in prison and you did not visit me." Then they also will answer, "Lord, when was it that we saw you hungry or thirsty or a stranger or naked or sick or in prison, and did not take care of you?" Then he will answer them, "Truly I tell you, just as you did not do it to one of the least of these, you did not do it to me." And these will go away into eternal punishment, but the righteous into eternal life.

MATTHEW 25:31-46

This passage reminds me that I'm not bothered so much by the Scripture verses I do not understand. Rather, the verses that I *do understand* terrify me—as a believer, a citizen, *and* a politician.

How will our nation fare if we are judged on whether we feed the hungry, give drink to the thirsty, welcome strangers, clothe the naked, treat the sick, and visit the prisoners? Worse yet, this is how the Lord Jesus himself says, explicitly and clearly, we will be judged. One does not have to draw principles and argue much over applications. Few of us measure up well by Jesus' standards.

NO NEW ISSUES

I remember talking with a fellow state legislator years ago. My friend, a veteran of many years in the legislature, said to me as a new legislator, "You know, Roy, there aren't any new bills. There are the same issues. Sometimes little differences, little refinements. But the same issues. The same bills."

That was true for the two *decades* he served.

More than that, it has been true for the two *millennia* since Jesus served.

The day after the fellow legislator and I talked, I considered Matthew 25 and noted the following actions of the people that Jesus said will be "blessed by my Father [and] inherit the kingdom prepared for [them] from the foundation of the world."

"I WAS HUNGRY AND YOU GAVE ME FOOD."

A few years ago, when my wife, Nancy, asked a group of kids at a local community center whether they were excited about Christmas vacation, they told her no. Surprised, Nancy asked why not. "We won't get to eat," they said.

The Tennessee legislature passed a bill requiring breakfasts to be served in certain schools that had many low-income students. Teachers tell me the meals at school are all some children get. Thank God some of them get two meals a day now, at least on weekdays.

In my district, an elderly gentleman back then told me, "As best I can tell, most of the older folks around here get Social Security checks of about $300 per month. And that sales tax of 7.5 percent may not be much to some, but to someone on $300 per month, that's almost $25. And sometimes that $25 in sales tax means they can't afford enough food."

"I WAS THIRSTY AND YOU GAVE ME SOMETHING TO DRINK."

A legislative colleague and I talked about the destruction of the river bottomlands—the killing of the timber around the rivers. He told me he had never been much of a conservationist or environmentalist. But he said he understood that those same bottoms once served as natural filters, removing chemicals and pollutants. But no longer. The water now runs off quickly into our streams, and our water grows more contaminated. If we think the $20 billion cleanwater bill was expensive, we may not have seen anything yet.

My colleague was concerned that some business owners are simply not honest about the waste they discharge. In fact, several businesses had recently been caught dumping chemicals and hazardous wastes in the Nashville area. "And if they're not doing right," my friend said, "we politicians are about the only folks who can stop them."

My colleague was right. But even more importantly, the only ones who can make politicians act are citizens.

If we don't keep our water supplies free from hazardous wastes, we will all be thirsty or, at best, paying through the teeth for clean water to drink.

"I WAS A STRANGER AND YOU WELCOMED ME."

Homeless citizens are all around us—in every large city and in most smaller ones. More than 800,000 Americans are homeless on any given day, including 200,000 children.[7] All of them are strangers to most of us.

Other strangers who need welcoming include abused women and children. One woman I talked with recently decided to do something for these strangers by starting a shelter for such victims.

The strangers most foreign to us are the immigrants and refugees who have recently arrived in this country. At a time when many cry out against them, perhaps we should remember that all of us except the Native Americans are either immigrants or descendants of immigrants.

"I WAS NAKED AND YOU GAVE ME CLOTHING."

For many years my hometown Rotary Club raised funds so that desperately needy children at Christmas could shop at two stores on the court square. They and their parents or guardians got to pick out thirty dollars' worth of clothes.

One December, eight-year-old Tommy came into the store. I went with him to pick out some shoes to replace his holey tennis shoes.

The problem was this: even when the first pair of shoes he tried on did not fit, he still did not want to take them off. When I finally got the appropriate-size shoes for him, I could not get him to take them off so he could try on some jeans.

Naked? Maybe not literally. But a boy whose shoes have more holes than shoe material and whose only pair of pants is ripped has great need—and the Bible directs us to help him.

"I WAS SICK AND YOU TOOK CARE OF ME."

As a lawyer, I once had a client whose elderly father was in a nursing home. When his arm accidently came to rest on a heater next to his bed, he was too weak to lift it. So it lay there. And lay there. Searing, stinking flesh. Third-degree burns.

Legislation eventually passed that gave the state adequate enforcement powers and authority to levy civil penalties on nursing homes endangering and harming citizens. More recently, after others died in a nursing home fire, we passed legislation to require sprinklers and smoke detectors in nursing homes.

"I WAS IN PRISON AND YOU VISITED ME."

A group from my church faithfully visits the local jail, offering prayers, Bible study, and a ministry of hospitality. They see it as a biblical mandate. After participating in these visits, group members came to believe that taxpayers could save large jail costs by investing in literacy, jobs, and affordable drug treatment.

For years, few citizens and even fewer officials visited one of Tennessee's prisons. Perhaps it should have been no surprise that the federal courts took over our corrections system. And how many of us have done better than those absentee citizens and officials? My legislative colleague says there really are not many new bills, and there really are not many new political issues. He is right. We are still far from resolving the issues Jesus set forth two thousand years ago.

THE GOOD NEWS

The Good News, the Gospel, is that you don't just work on these issues as Christian citizens to be *like* Jesus. You go to these people and work on these issues to be *with* Jesus.

"When did we see *you*, Jesus, hungry or thirsty, a stranger or naked, sick or in prison?" That is the question people who helped others will ask at the judgment. To which Jesus will reply, "Truly I tell you, just as you did it to

As a Christian citizen healing the wounds of our society—working for *shalom*—you will meet Jesus.

25

one of the least of these who are members of my family, you did it to me" (Matthew 25:40). As a Christian citizen healing the wounds of our society—working for *shalom*—you will meet Jesus.

POLITICS AS WORSHIP

When you feed the hungry and clothe the naked, you will not only meet Jesus; you can also worship God. This may seem hard to believe. Few people think of political engagement as a form of worship. And of course it is not always so. But before you dismiss the notion out of hand, hear the words of the prophet Micah, spoken 2,700 years ago:

> "With what shall I come before the Lord, and bow myself before God on high?
>
> Shall I come before him with burnt offerings, with calves a year old?
>
> Will the LORD be pleased with thousands of rams, with ten thousands of rivers of oil?
>
> Shall I give my firstborn for my transgression, the fruit of my body for the sin of my soul?"
>
> He has told you, O mortal, what is good; and what does the Lord require of you

but to do justice, and to love kindness, and to walk
humbly with your God?

MICAH 6:6-8

Micah is asking how he should worship God. He considers the
traditional forms of worship—sacrifice of animals and offering of
goods. He raises the possibility of dedicating his very flesh and blood.
But then he concludes that these are not the best forms of worship.
Rather, God requires three things of us: doing justice, loving
kindness, and walking humbly. These requirements have distinct
political implications. We cannot fully do justice in our society
without acting politically. And kindness and humility are much more
powerful concepts than simply being nice; like justice, they should
have a public as well as a private expression. If these qualities mark
our politics, then politics can indeed be a form of worship.

CHAPTER 3

DOING JUSTICE

*Let justice roll down like waters, and righteousness like an
ever-flowing stream.*
Amos 5:24, RSV

*Righteousness exalts a nation, but sin is a reproach to any
people.*
Proverbs 14:34

*Lord, we know that you'll be comin' through this line
today. So help us to treat you well.*
Food line volunteer

One simple way of expressing a Christian understanding of
politics is to point out that politics and society should reflect
the character of God. To answer the question, "what is faithful
politics?" one should ask the question, "what is God like?"

One characteristic of God is a love of justice. God does not just have
an affection for justice; God demands it. Because God is just, God
insists that society also be just.

Justice touches many areas of our lives. In the Bible, justice
repeatedly is tied to economic issues, specifically to the plight of the
poor. Some poverty the Bible blames on individual shortcomings:
laziness, failure to plan, drunkenness, and the like (e.g., Proverbs
20:4; 21:25; 23:20-21). Often, however, the Bible reveals poverty as
the result of society's failure to ensure justice (e.g., Isaiah 58:6-12;
Jeremiah 22:13-16; Amos 5:11-12).

When a society is not just, everyone suffers, not only the poor. (See Jeremiah 5:26-29, among many other verses.) God's anger at the failure to ensure justice, often represented by the oppression of the poor, leads to punishment for the entire society, rich and poor alike. Simple self-interest, even without a passion for righteousness, compels us to put justice at the top of the political agenda.

JUSTICE EXALTS A NATION

I once was asked to speak on the idea expressed in Proverbs 14:34 that "righteousness exalts a nation."[1] The Hebrew term *tsedaqah*, rendered "righteousness" in most English translations, is closely tied to the concept of justice. In fact, in other Old Testament passages, *tsedaqah* is accurately rendered as "justice" (see Deuteronomy 33:21, NASB, NKJV, NLT; Job 8:3, NKJV), and a case can be made for doing so in Proverbs 14:34 as well. Similarly, the Greek word *dikaiosune*, often rendered "righteousness" in English translations of the New Testament, is at times more accurately translated as "justice" (see Acts 17:31, NIV, NLT; Hebrews 11:33, ESV, NIV, NLT; Revelation 19:11, NLT). In these verses, and in many others throughout Scripture, the implication is clear: Righteousness and justice are inseparably linked; a nation that ignores or undermines justice will not be exalted by God, only disgraced (Proverbs 14:34).[2]

As John Donahue observes, "In God justice and mercy are not in opposition."[3] Instead, as Abraham Heschel taught, "God is compassion without compromise; justice, though not inclemency."[4]

The compassionate nature of biblical justice is clearly seen in the tremendous amount of attention the Bible gives to the treatment of the poor. In Proverbs 14:31 we are warned, "Those who oppress the poor insult their Maker, but those who are kind to the needy honor him." A society cannot ignore the plight of the poor and call itself just or righteous. True justice—the justice of God—is compassionate. This is the justice that exalts nations—the kind of justice that politics must work to ensure.

> Throughout Scripture, the implication is clear: Righteousness and justice are inseparably linked; a nation that ignores or undermines justice will not be exalted by God, only disgraced.

Most political debates center on legislation or public policies. These political debates about laws usually seem far removed from the Bible. In our pluralistic society with so many different beliefs, public debates typically emphasize secular reasoning and arguments. But for Christians seeking to learn what God would have us do, Scripture is always relevant and even central. Biblical law can be particularly helpful as we shape American law.

In ancient Israel, awareness of God entailed awareness of Israel's own poverty and the death that awaited it unless God actively intervened. God rescued a landless, enslaved people and gave Israel "a land flowing with milk and honey" (Deuteronomy 26:9). This fundamental understanding Israel had of itself, that it had been rescued from slavery,

> Politics must work to ensure compassionate justice.

gave the people sympathy with the poor and abandoned.

Israel's self-understanding was, like life itself, inescapably connected with the land. Israel's laws reflected the people's experiences of poverty and their connectedness with the land. When they were the landless poor in Egypt, God rescued them. When there were still landless poor in Israel, God's laws protected them.

JUSTICE: WHAT DOES BIBLICAL LAW SAY ABOUT THE POOR?

In the Old Testament, justice was fidelity to the threefold relationship with God, others, and the land.[5] In a nomadic civilization, families may have been richer or poorer, but the tribe was not divided into different social classes.[6] Even slaves were not a separate class; they also formed part of the family. So it likely was with Israel because the people were seminomadic, moving about the land.

Settlement, however, brought a "profound social transformation."[7] Israel's laws reflected its historical experience. As the poor and landless increasingly suffered, laws were developed to provide increased protection for them.

By exploring how ancient Israel's laws sought to achieve justice, we will see how the Bible calls us to do justice today.

PREDATORY LENDING

Israel's earliest laws forbade the exaction of interest from a poor person and required a creditor to return before sundown a neighbor's garment that had been pledged (see Exodus 22:25-27).

In ancient times, commercial relations were comparatively undeveloped, but loans were commonly needed for the purpose of relieving distress. To exact interest from a borrower who was reduced to poverty by misfortune and debt was to gain from a neighbor's need.[8] Thus, the Pentateuch, the first five books of the Bible, condemned the charging of interest from fellow Israelites (see Deuteronomy 23:19-20).

Despite Nehemiah's and Ezekiel's calls for strict observance of these laws, violations were frequent (see Nehemiah 5:6-13; Ezekiel 18:8-17; 22:12). The practice of Israelites lending to fellow Israelites at exorbitant rates became "a social plague" that made debtors' situations practically hopeless.[9]

Today, poor and indebted Americans are the victims of a similar social plague. One contemporary abuse of working people and senior citizens is predatory lending.

Loaning people money to buy homes is an honorable profession. But tricking people into predatory loans in order to take their homes from them is dastardly.

Predators target the most trusting and, therefore, the most vulnerable in our society and use deceptive tactics, including high-pressure schemes, to keep victims from properly understanding loan terms. Often they promise one set of terms but formalize another set. Borrowers learn the truth too late.

> Predators target the most vulnerable in our society and use deceptive tactics to rob them.

A Memphis couple, for example, was deceived about the interest rate on their loans, one of which had a rate of 29 percent. Another woman was pressured into taking out a $35,000 loan that included an 18 percent interest rate, more than $2,000 in loan origination fees, and a $6,000 credit life-insurance premium. Since her loan was negatively amortized, she owed more than the original loan even after six years of paying $500 a month.

A mentally and physically impaired World War II veteran was deceived when a loan solicitor visited the disabled man's home, brought beer and cigarettes, and pressured him to refinance his mortgage. The loan included a misleading promissory note, more than $3,000 in fees, and a mortgage balance $9,000 higher than the original with monthly payments that exceeded 40 percent of his income.

All these are cases where politics and politicians could and should do something. They can protect people from predators who would legally rob them.

We often complain of being overregulated, and in some areas we are. But the Bible is filled with regulations about how people should deal with each other— including economic regulations—in order to live justly. Those who claim to follow the Bible should insist on the same today.

LAWS PROTECTING WORKERS

The poor in our society commonly are stereotyped as lazy. But in the Bible, as in much of the world today, the poor work the toughest jobs, often for the longest hours. So it makes sense that God, in his concern for the poor, also defends the rights of workers. Deuteronomy, for instance, extends protections not only to the poor, but it also asserts rights protecting workers from oppressive employers (see Deuteronomy 24:14-15).

The life of a laborer was hard. Unjust masters often failed to give wage earners their due, so the law required that they be paid each evening because the wage earner "is poor, and sets his heart upon it" (Deuteronomy 24:15, RSV). Even so, the law repeatedly was flouted, and the prophets condemned the foul practice of the disobedient employer "who makes his neighbors work for nothing, and does not give them their wages" (Jeremiah 22:13; see also Malachi 3:5).

We face similar issues today. We wrestle with issues like minimum wage, workplace safety, and worker health benefits. Not long ago, some of us in the Tennessee legislature fought to make sure that when factories closed, the dislocated workers' families could qualify for affordable health insurance. Another time we worked to see that workers exposed to dangerous chemicals had a right to know exactly what they were handling.

The temptation to treat others unfairly to increase one's wealth is a timeless part of fallen human nature, and so is the temptation to cheat one's employer by not working hard. But God recognizes that the employer most often has the greater power to do harm, so most of God's biblical requirements are aimed at those with the most power.

AID TO THE POOR, THE WIDOW, AND THE FATHERLESS

In ancient Israel, provisions were made for direct aid to the poor. The law forbade gleaning by the landowner. Gleaning was the practice of gathering or picking up what was left in the field after the harvest (see Deuteronomy 24:19-22). The landowners were forbidden from taking every last bit of the land's output for their own benefit. The owner was prevented from cleaning up the field, from claiming what remained in "a grasping spirit."[10] Instead, the remains of the harvest were left for the widow, the fatherless, the sojourner, and the poor (see Leviticus 19:9-10, RSV; Deuteronomy 24:19, RSV).

> The temptation to treat others unfairly to increase one's wealth is a timeless part of fallen human nature.

Deuteronomic law also attempted to meet the needs of the poor by requiring landowners to tithe from their land.[11] The tithe was a tenth of the land's yield and was to be used for an annual meal in which everyone shared and, every third year, as an offering for charitable purposes. This tithe was to be distributed to those who had no land on which to produce crops. The tithe acknowledged God's ownership of the land and its fruits. It was a means of support for those in need.[12]

How are ancient laws that prohibited gleaning and required tithing relevant to us today? The urban poor, for example, can hardly glean from rural farms and vineyards. And yet the principle remains the same. The Bible forbids those of us who have resources from keeping everything for ourselves. To do so is to make the mistake of thinking that everything we have is the result of our own efforts and belongs to us, rather than seeing it as a gift from God that ultimately belongs to God.

> The Bible forbids those of us who have resources from keeping everything for ourselves.

Of course, we have government programs helping those in need: aid to the poor and hungry, relief for the widow and fatherless, Social Security, Medicare, Medicaid, school lunch programs. Some—including many Christians—even think government is doing too much.

But if we think some are doing too much, or that current efforts are wasteful or promote bad habits, it is not enough to criticize those efforts. It is our responsibility, if we claim to seek guidance from the Bible, to meet those needs ourselves or to insist on political action that does so. If churches and government are not correctly serving the truly needy and vulnerable, we need to do better. But doing nothing is not a biblical option.

I have a devout friend who not only knows biblical principles but acts on them. Kim works as a housekeeper and child-care provider. She insists on knowing the gross amount of her pay so she can be sure to tithe fully. She takes in—literally—those in great need, and she helps all she sees who are hurting. What would our country be like if every Christian did like Kim? How much government could be eliminated if Christians followed her example and churches really reached out to love and serve as Christ taught?

God's concern for justice is relevant to many other issues in politics today. At the core of most of those issues are the ideas that everything ultimately belongs to God and that vulnerable people need protection and hope.

The Bible calls for both people and property to be treated rightly. People who owned land—and who owned slaves—were required to acknowledge their responsibilities to both. Hebrew slaves could not be kept for more than six years without their consent (see Exodus 21:2-6). The land was to be given a rest from planting every seventh year. Debtors were to have their debts forgiven from time to time.

Every fifty years, land was to be returned to the families who sold it. Strangers and foreigners were to be treated respectfully and fairly (see Leviticus 25:3-4, 28; 19:34; Deuteronomy 15:1-2).

Some debate how or even whether the people of Israel obeyed these commands. But the biblical intent is clear. Society should be structured so that wealth and power do not all flow permanently into the hands of a few. Those in need should be helped, and the poor should be able to see that there is a way out of poverty.

The Gospels also contain numerous references to the plight of the poor and our responsibility for it. Consider the painful story of the political leader whom Jesus addresses in Luke:

> A certain ruler asked him, "Good Teacher, what must I do to inherit eternal life?" Jesus said to him, "Why do you call me good? No one is good but God alone. You know the commandments: 'You shall not commit adultery; You shall not murder; You shall not steal; You shall not bear false witness; Honor your father and mother.'" He replied, "I have kept all these since my youth." When Jesus heard this, he said to him, "There is still one thing lacking. Sell all that you own and distribute the money to the poor, and you will have treasure in heaven; then come, follow me." But when he heard this, he became sad; for he was very rich. Jesus looked at him and said, "How hard it is for those who have wealth to enter the kingdom of God! Indeed, it is

easier for a camel to go through the eye of a needle than for someone who is rich to enter the kingdom of God."

LUKE 18:18-25

Jesus warns that the temptation to hold power and wealth is great—so great that we're often willing to sacrifice anything, including our own salvation, to preserve it. Fortunately, the passage ends with this exchange between Jesus and the crowd: "Those who heard it said, 'Then who can be saved?' He replied, 'What is impossible for mortals is possible for God'" (Luke 18:26-27).

CHARITY AND JUSTICE

The world of the Bible is not our world, but certain constants remain. Exploitation and greed are still part of human nature. The poor and needy, as Jesus knew, are still with us. Laws, and the political system which creates them, can protect the vulnerable and poor. The creation, execution, and enforcement of such laws is what politics at its biblical best is about.

> The Bible calls us to shape our society in such a way that the poor are provided for and justice is ensured.

The Bible calls us to shape our society in such a way that the poor are provided for and justice is ensured. This is to be a matter of basic political and social structure, not something left to individual charity and to chance. Justice is the opportunity to buy a home and build equity, not just a bed in an emergency shelter. Justice is access to the education and job skills that enable you to feed your family, not just food baskets at Christmas. Justice understands the old saying, "Give a man a fish and you feed him for a day. Teach a man to fish and you feed him for a lifetime."

Professor John Donahue observed that Martin Luther "translated the God of justice into a God of love. The task of our age may well be the reverse—to translate the love of God into the doing of justice."[13]

CHAPTER 4

PROTECTING LIFE

I have set before you life and death, blessings and curses.
Choose life so that you and your descendants may live.
DEUTERONOMY 30:19

If one characteristic of God is a love of justice, another is a love of life. In the New Testament, Jesus identifies himself as "the bread of life" (John 6:35) and "the resurrection and the life" (John 11:25). In the Old Testament, God speaks through Moses and commands the people to "choose life" (Deuteronomy 30:19).

But what does it mean to "choose life"? In Deuteronomy, life is linked to law. Throughout the first five books of the Bible, God instructs God's people in how they must live to be in the right relationship with God and with each other—to establish *shalom*.

LAW, BLESSING, AND LIFE

For Christians, law does not save us, but it does protect us. God's law is the working out in practice of God's compassion and justice. God's law provides operating instructions from the One who made us and knows how we work. The link between obedience to God's law and blessing runs throughout Scripture. Just a few verses before the command in Deuteronomy to choose life, we find the following: "If you obey the commandments of the Lord your God that I am commanding you today, by loving the Lord your God, walking in his ways, and observing his commandments, decrees, and ordinances, then you shall live and become numerous, and the Lord your God will bless you in the land that you are entering to possess" (Deuteronomy 30:16).

This vision of the link between law and blessing should be a charge to lawmakers, public servants, and all who participate in politics. Ours is a God of life, not death. As God's children, we have a responsibility to protect and nurture life. Faithful politics requires us to support laws and policies that protect lives, especially the lives of those least able to protect themselves.

The following are stories of laws created to protect life. Behind the lifesaving laws were people of faith who, through their political involvement, literally saved hundreds, if not thousands, of lives.

TEEN DRUNK DRIVERS

Drunk drivers have killed too many of my friends.

There was Mike, the guy a little older than me in school who picked me for his baseball, basketball, and football teams, even though I wasn't very good and the other side did not want me. And because he believed in me, I became a better player.

Unfortunately, he also believed in one of his buddies who had too much to drink one night and went off the road. Mike was killed.

As a state senator, Roy worked with police and citizens to increase penalties for drunk driving and possession and distribution of the illegal drug crystal meth. Roy also sponsored legislation to monitor sex offenders and put sexual predators in jail.

Two other friends, one a star athlete and another the manager of our high school basketball team, were always nice to me at a time when we freshmen players did not receive an abundance of kindness from other seniors. Then one night they were drinking and driving. They drove off the road and crashed. Flames consumed the car and their bodies. They were identified only by their dental records.

A younger friend, also drunk, drove off the road one winter night. Instead of burning up, he froze to death.

And these are just a few of the ones I knew personally.

What can anyone do about drunk driving? The people and the politicians can do something. Government can work to save lives.

The Tennessee legislature passed legislation that set a lower, tougher, zero tolerance standard for young people driving and drinking. We also passed legislation to do something about convicted drunk drivers who were going years without serving their sentences. We also gave judges the power to order ignition interlocks on cars to keep drunk drivers from driving while intoxicated.

Have we managed to eliminate drunk driving? No. But are fewer dying because of these acts? Absolutely. People are alive today because of politics.

TEENS AND GUNS

If teenagers have long had a problem with alcohol, they now have another deadly problem—guns. A teenager in my district shot another teen with a pistol at the county fair. The county official who told me about the incident has three sons, like I do. He urged me, "You need to do something before one of our boys gets killed."

So I sponsored a bill passed by the legislature that, for the first time in Tennessee history, prohibits juveniles from packing pistols. It may yet save someone's life.

CATCHING KILLERS

Jennifer Melton was about to begin her senior year in high school. One morning after Jennifer's parents had gone to work, a man came into their home. He raped Jennifer and shot her in the head.

There was a time during that murder investigation when electronic surveillance—a wiretap—of the prime suspect might have solved that case. It could have taken the murderer off the streets, potentially saving some other young woman's life.

But Tennessee was one of about ten states that did not allow state law enforcement to work with prosecutors—under the supervision of judges—to conduct electronic surveillance, even in murder cases.

The legislature changed that. Now law enforcement officers are beginning to solve murders that previously went unsolved and left the killers at large and the public in danger. A police lieutenant with whom I worked to pass this legislation told me that one electronic surveillance alone, made possible by this law, resulted in an indictment in a murder case that previously had been beyond the grasp of authorities. It also made possible another twenty-one indictments of major drug pushers.

DOMESTIC VIOLENCE

Sometimes people even need protection from those with whom they live. Twice as many women are murdered by their husbands or boyfriends as by strangers.[1] Hospital emergency department records show that 39 percent of violence-related injuries are inflicted on females. Eighty-four percent of those treated are injured by intimates.[2]

I once stood in a county courtroom and looked at the most bruised face I have ever seen. The woman's face was literally black and blue.

> Domestic violence is the only crime where the victim goes home to live with the criminal.

Later in the hallway as I walked past the bruised woman, she spoke to me. When I heard her say my name, I recognized her voice. I had represented her and her daughter when her first husband had been accidentally killed. She had been in my office, in my home, and I knew her voice—but I could not recognize her face.

Her beating had come at the hands of her new husband. It was not the first time she had been beaten by him. But it took injuries that required a trip to the hospital before an arrest came—and the violence stopped.

Domestic violence is the only crime where the victim goes home to live with the criminal. And too often the victim finds herself (occasionally himself) trapped not only with the criminal but also with the weapon that the criminal used to threaten or injure her.

My colleagues and I passed a bill that requires law enforcement officers, when they have probable cause, to arrest these violent abusers. Furthermore, it authorizes law enforcement to remove weapons used in the violent crime or that the officer believes will endanger the officer or others.

Studies have shown that when police arrest an abuser, domestic violence decreases substantially. We can't entirely stop people from abusing those they live with, but politics can do some things to try to restore *shalom* to their homes.

ORGAN TRANSPLANTS

Not all the laws that protect people have to do with criminal behavior. Sometimes faithful politics can help save the lives of the sick.

For example, my former legislative assistant, Linda, needed liver and kidney transplants. Without them, it was just a question of time until the dialysis and her body failed.

My friend and constituent, Don, needed a heart transplant. Without it, he too would die.

But there are too few organs donated. More people with failing organs need transplants than there are organs to be transplanted.

So the legislature worked with the Department of Safety, eventually securing its cooperation to pass legislation that lets citizens indicate on their driver's license that they wish to donate their organs.

I saw my friend Don not long ago with his new heart—he was celebrating the Fourth of July at a carnival. I see Linda frequently during the legislative sessions—serving and doing well with her new liver and kidney. Don and Linda are alive because people donated their organs and gave them life.

SAFETY SEATS FOR INFANTS AND SEAT BELTS FOR CHILDREN

A woman came to a legislative hearing and spoke to us. She told the story of her family driving on vacation when someone crashed into them. One of her children, the one with her the day she testified, had been in a child safety seat. But her other child had not been protected properly. That child she buried.

A child unprotected by a safety seat is eleven times more likely to be killed in a serious car wreck.[3]

In the two years before that woman's testimony, thirty-six infants and toddlers died on Tennessee highways. Five of them were in safety seats, but the crashes simply were not survivable. Almost all of the other thirty-one, however, would have survived if they had been in safety seats.[4] Furthermore, for each child killed in a car wreck, another seventeen were permanently disabled.[5]

That meant that on average in Tennessee, a child under four was either killed or permanently disabled almost every single day, approximately 90 percent of them needlessly because they were not protected. That is why we now require every child under four to be protected in a safety seat.

Then there are the children a little older, like Karen.

Karen was a nine-year-old when I first met her. She and her sister had just come to live with my friends, her adoptive parents, having been removed from a home where they both had suffered terrible abuse.

A few hours after we met, the family was driving across west Tennessee when their van hit a puddle of water, hydroplaned, and went into a concrete bridge. Karen was in the very rear and did not have her safety belt on. The wreck severely damaged her spinal cord.

Without her adoptive parents knowing it, Karen had slipped her safety belt off. No law will stop that. But until recently Tennessee law permitted children over four who were not in the front seat to be unprotected. Now it at least requires all children up to age thirteen to be belted safely.

These laws will keep many children out of wheelchairs, unlike Karen. For others, the laws will keep them out of a premature grave.

PRIMARY CARE

Laws can prevent and punish; they can also encourage. One thing I have tried to encourage as a state legislator is more health care for people in places doctors sometimes don't want to go. Both rural and inner-city America need primary health care, but it is too often absent. It can make the difference between life and death.

I know this firsthand because my father came within ten minutes of dying when I was barely a teenager. That is what the doctor who saved him told my mother. Ten minutes. That was the difference in my having or not having a father through high school and college.

That is one personal reason I joined with others in pushing legislation to train and attract more primary care physicians to serve in rural areas and inner cities. That is why we sponsored legislation to see nurse- practitioners reimbursed for serving the poor and to empower other health care professionals to serve where physicians will not or cannot.

The biblical story of the Good Samaritan is, in part, a story about health care. If we miss that practical point, we miss the point of what it means to be a good neighbor. Political action can help us fulfill one of the central commands of our faith.

WHISTLE-BLOWERS

Sometimes all politicians have to do is protect someone who wants to do the right thing. I recall a man who came to my law office early one morning and told me an unbelievable tale. He said he worked for a public utility that was endangering thousands of lives by failing to obey safety regulations.

> Sometimes all politicians have to do is protect someone who wants to do the right thing.

The gas company was failing to pressure-test gas lines, which could then leak and blow up. The company was ignoring broken cutoff valves that would not cut off gas in an emergency, which might mean an entire complex or area could be torched in a fire. And where the leaks were so bad that citizens complained about the smell, the company had quit putting odorant in the gas. The gas was still leaking, but now there was nothing to warn of the danger.

The story of a company imperiling so many people was so far-fetched that I did not believe the man at first. But he seemed sincere. He said he wanted to keep people from dying, but he also wanted to keep his job and support his family, and he was afraid he would be fired for reporting the illegal activities. I assured him that I thought the law would protect him but told him I would check. To my surprise, I found he had no legal protection, even for telling the truth about the illegal acts.

On his behalf, I called the Public Service Commission without revealing his name. The commission levied the largest fine in its history—and ordered the dangers corrected.

The Tennessee General Assembly then passed a law that protects honest workers who refuse to participate in crimes or who blow the whistle on illegal acts performed by their employer. The law also protects honest businesses that obey the law so they can compete on a fair playing field.

Most importantly, the law saves the lives of those who would have been endangered by illegal activities that would not have been reported because honest workers feared losing their jobs.

ABORTION AND CAPITAL PUNISHMENT

When many think about protecting life, they think first—and sometimes only—about abortion. For these devout citizens, millions of abortions are a contemporary Holocaust against innocent and defenseless children. They cry out for laws to protect the unborn.

Despite a doctor's recommendation, the Herrons refused to abort a risky pregnancy. Now they are blessed with twin sons. Roy voted to ban partial-birth abortion and all abortions except for victims of rape, incest and when the mother's life is in danger.

Some faithful who abhor abortions, however, do not want government taking decisions away from innocent victims and their pastors and doctors in cases of incest or rape or when a woman's life truly is threatened by pregnancy.

Other Christians acknowledge that each abortion is a tragedy, but they fear that the unintended consequences of prohibition also are tragic. They talk of back-alley butchers and focus on women facing unwanted pregnancies.

Some Christians, particularly many Roman Catholics, talk about life as a "seamless garment" and oppose both abortion and the death penalty. They advocate what they call "a consistent pro-life ethic" and argue against taking lives, whether in the womb or in prison.

With documented cases of innocent persons sentenced to die, some Christians argue that life sentences, particularly life without parole, can protect us without risking the killing of innocents. They point to the New Testament and the teachings of Jesus to argue against capital punishment.

But most Americans see capital punishment as society's just act of self-defense when used against those who have willfully taken human life. Relying principally on the Old Testament, many Christians justify the death penalty as biblical. They believe capital punishment can be a life-saving deterrent.

Both abortion and capital punishment have spawned countless books and articles, as well as judicial decisions. Whatever your views on abortion and capital punishment, you probably feel strongly. You most likely are willing to act on these issues to protect life.

But thousands of other lives also are at stake. Political decisions on many other issues determine whether people live or die.

SAVING LIVES

The well-known Scripture passage John 3:16 describes what God has done for us:

> For God so loved the world, that he gave his only begotten Son, that whosoever believeth in him should not perish, but have everlasting life.
>
> KJV

And 1 John 3:16 reveals what God wants us to do for one another:

> We know love by this, that he laid down his life for
> us—and we ought to lay down our lives for one another.

Our disgust over politics at its worst should not blind us to what politics at its best can do. Politics can save lives and give us an opportunity to "lay down our lives for one another."

The Herron family in 2004: Rick, Nancy, Roy, Ben and John.

Roy with his 93-year-old mother, Mary Cornelia.

Roy's dad returned from World War II a wounded veteran. He went to law school on the GI Bill and became a judge.

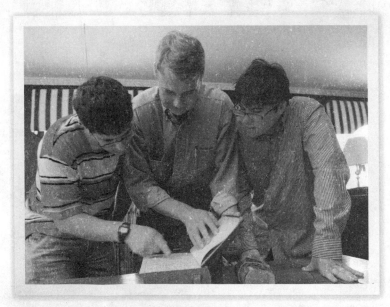

The Herron family Bible dates from the mid-1800s. After 150+ years, it is quite fragile, but its message still rings clear. Roy wrote and sponsored the Bible in Schools Act that enables public school students to study the Bible. He also wrote and sponsored the Student Religious Liberty Act that protects students' right to pray in schools.

Roy and his bride, Nancy, on their wedding day in 1987.

Roy visits with friends at the First Methodist Church of Dresden where Roy once served as a minister.

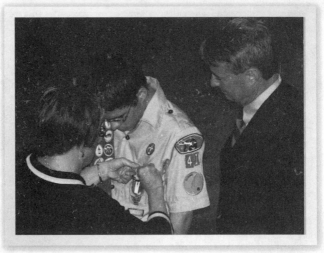

Roy's son, John, receives his Eagle Scout award. John is one of seven Herrons to become an Eagle Scout, including both of his brothers and Roy.

Roy and his sons enjoy hunting and shooting. Roy grew up hunting with his father and brothers. Because he wants to protect such family traditions for future generations, Roy helped sponsor and pass the Tennessee Right to Hunt and Fish constitutional amendment.

As a part-time legislator, Roy has held more than 1,000 listening meetings to hear the concerns of the people he represents so he can represent their views and values.

As a state legislator, Roy Herron has missed only one session - the day his youngest son, Ben, was being born.

Roy, Nancy and their three sons have attended public schools. Roy is a graduate of UT Martin. As a Rotary Fellow, he studied New Testament and Ethics, then graduated with degrees in law and divinity.

Roy enjoys a half-marathon with his son, Rick. Roy has completed more than 30 marathons and three 140-mile Ironman triathlons.

Roy and Nancy share a laugh. They've been married 23 years.

Roy on the farm he and his family own. His family started farming in Weakley County before Davy Crockett arrived in the 1820s.

Roy is conservative with money. His pickup truck now has 400,000 miles. Roy's truck, Nancy's van, and the car their three sons share together have over 700,000 miles.

Roy helped lead the fight to fix TennCare while working to protect those who really need help.

CHAPTER 5

DEFENDING FREEDOM

*I am the Lord, and I will free you from the burdens of
the Egyptians and deliver you from slavery to them. I
will redeem you with an outstretched arm and with
mighty acts of judgment. I will take you as my people,
and I will be your God.*
EXODUS 6:6-7

*For freedom Christ has set us free. Stand firm, therefore,
and do not submit again to a yoke of slavery.*
GALATIANS 5:1

You will know the truth, and the truth will make you free.
JOHN 8:32

Freedoms come in many shapes and sizes. Among them are political and spiritual freedoms. God's *shalom* is concerned with both, and so is faithful politics.

Political freedom consists of the liberties that citizens demand from their government. For example, in American democracy citizens are guaranteed the rights to speak openly and to worship God as they choose, not as the president or majority political party demands. It is important to understand that political freedom, as important as it is, is not the same as spiritual freedom and that political freedom alone is not enough to create the kind of society God wants for us.

Spiritual freedom is the freedom that comes from being in right relationship to God. It is experiencing *shalom* and liberation through

> Political freedom consists of the liberties that citizens demand from their government.

> Spiritual freedom is the freedom that comes from being in right relationship to God.

the holy power and presence of God. It is repairing the damage of sin and human fallenness. The Bible speaks of sin as a form of slavery and bondage (see John 8:33-34, RSV). There is a link between law—moral and otherwise—and freedom. Old Testament scholar Walter Harrelson calls the Ten Commandments "Israel's great charter of freedom."[1] He argues, "The first thing people need to know is that they can have no real life, no real freedom, no real joy in life save as they lay aside the kinds of action that destroy the very things they are seeking. The Ten Commandments ward off conduct on our part which, if engaged in, will make impossible the love of God and of neighbor."[2]

Spiritual freedom is primary for people of faith, but political freedom is not insignificant. Without political freedom, believers cannot worship as God calls them to, pray or read the Bible as they wish, sing joyful praises, or come together as a faith community, at least not without persecution. Without political freedom, people of faith are hindered from fully exploring their deepest yearning for ultimate freedom in God.

Perhaps this is one reason God rescued his people from oppression so long ago.

THE KING WHO WOULDN'T LET THE PEOPLE GO

When our twins were about three years old, my wife started a tradition. One evening during the Christmas season, after the boys were bathed and wrestled into pajamas, Nancy said, "Let's light the Advent candle!"

We all went to the foyer of our home. Nancy lit the candles that swayed unsteadily on a homemade wreath on a cabinet. I brought the quilt from my grandfather's tattered chair in the library and spread it on the cold, marblelike floor. Then we sat on the quilt with me holding the two boys and their children's Bible. The candles provided barely enough light for Nancy to read us a Bible story.

Night after night, the boys chose stories for us to read to them, determined in part, it seemed, by the beautiful watercolors of various people and scenes from the Bible. When we finished one story, the boys would squeal, "Let's read another!"

We started this during Advent, but even when Advent was a distant memory in the liturgical year, in the evenings one of our boys would still exclaim, "Let's do Advent!"

As weeks passed, the boys focused on one particular story. Resisting attempts to steer them to another story, they repeatedly pleaded,

"Let's read about the king that wouldn't let the people go!"

And we would read yet again the story of the rescue of Israel from Egypt, complete with its plagues and stubborn pharaoh.

After reading the description of each plague, I would read in a deeper voice the words of Moses to the king:

"Let my people go!"

Then the boys would recite the refrain:

"But the king just said, 'No!'"

Until, finally, finally, the people were allowed to flee to freedom.[3]

> Do children love so much to hear about the Exodus because all hearts, even young hearts, long for freedom?

What was it that attracted our three-and later four-year old boys to this story of the Exodus? Was it simply those vibrant watercolors of sick animals, people with sores, locusts in the air, blood in the river? Or was it just that little boys think plagues are marvelous? Did they hear about all these extraordinary things and become captured by the power—indeed, the miracle—that was described?

Their father, still much a little boy himself, is inclined to think it was the watercolors and the "neat plagues." Their mother thinks her smart sons simply discerned the fundamental nature of this central event in the history of the people of Israel.

Do children love so much to hear about the Exodus because all hearts, even young hearts, long for freedom?

EASTERN EUROPE AND COMMUNISM

We have seen a version of the Exodus story in our own times. For most of the twentieth century, the heavy hand of Communist oppression lay on Russia and Eastern Europe. Americans were fortunate to be free. But many of us take that freedom for granted. I only began to really appreciate freedom when I met people who were denied it.

Young Americans consider the Iron Curtain and Communism ancient history. But many of us grew up with bomb shelters, the Cold War, the Korean and Vietnamese wars, the crushing of freedom in Eastern Europe by Russian tanks and troops. To us, Communism was fearfully strong and the Iron Curtain frighteningly real. Unreal, until fairly recently, was the dream of freedom for those trapped in Communist countries.

In the late seventies, a divinity school classmate, my younger brother, and I traveled for six weeks in Eastern Europe. We went because we wanted to learn about oppression in countries behind the Iron Curtain. But the lessons we learned taught us as much about freedoms in our own country.

In Czechoslovakia we met a university student whose English was better than our own. We enjoyed a lighthearted conversation walking about his campus. When we stopped and sat down, I asked, "Was it better before 1968 or is it better now?"

Although he had understood my Tennessee twang until then, suddenly he did not seem to understand. I posed the question again in more detail:

"Was it better before 1968 when the Russians with their troops and tanks crushed the Dubcek government, or is it better now?"

Our friend again said he did not understand, but I noticed he kept glancing over his shoulder at two men leaning against a wall. The two were gazing at the sky, saying nothing.

Suddenly our friend got up and said he would walk us toward our campsite. Though we were not ready to go, we followed him. Two hundred yards away, he explained: "I could not talk there. They were listening."

"Would you get in trouble," I asked, "if you criticized your government or the Soviet Union?"

Our friend nodded. Though he lacked only a year to complete his academic program, he explained that for such an offense he could be expelled from the university. Forever. He also would be banned from holding many jobs, especially the good-paying ones.

I then went through a mental checklist of First Amendment freedoms. So much for freedom of speech. What about freedom of assembly?

Our friend explained that he secretly met with a group of students who criticized the government and talked about changes that needed to be made. If the government knew of their meetings, harsh measures would have been taken. He said they did not even tell one another their names, for fear that anyone caught and pressured would reveal the others' names.

> If the government knew of their meetings, harsh measures would have been taken.

I did not think it necessary to ask about the right to "petition the government for a redress of grievances."

Freedom of the press?

My friend shook his head. Before the Russians came in 1968, the press was not so restricted. But now, he told us, the media prints and broadcasts what the government orders. And the government, unlike before, strictly follows the orders of the Soviet Union.

Freedom of religion?

Our friend said he knew a Christian. One. No, not someone at the university, since Christians were not allowed to attend universities. But he did know a Christian.

Later, we met a few of these rare people ourselves.

My hometown is Dresden, Tennessee—named after Dresden, East Germany—so we visited my hometown's namesake. In Dresden we discovered a prayer meeting of thirty college-age Christians who were students at a technical school. They said they were permitted to learn trade skills, but the government would not let them attend a university.

We asked, "Why not?"

They replied, "Because we are Christians."

In Dresden we also met an older Christian, a schoolteacher. He said the government prohibited Christians from teaching school. Only because of a bureaucratic oversight, or perhaps a sympathetic government official, was he still teaching.

The struggle between church and government was most powerfully symbolized in East Berlin. Just passing through the military checkpoint at the Berlin Wall was frightening.

A huge communications tower dominated the city. A tremendously tall, thin concrete structure with a big ball near its top, it looked something like the Space Needle in Seattle, Washington. We walked around inside the ball with dozens of other tourists and viewed the city.

The tower was a showpiece symbolizing modern, technological, and atheistic East Germany. The government sold little replicas of the tower in the souvenir shops.

A few hundred feet away, almost in the tower's shadow, we found a centuries-old church. During our few days in East Berlin, we had seen the ruins of several churches destroyed in World War II. But this was the only church we found open. We walked inside, where we met three young Christians. The fathers of two were ministers, and all three were studying to become church workers. One noticed the cross I was wearing. She pointed to it and smiled. That was how our friendship began.

> The struggle between church and government was most powerfully symbolized in East Berlin.

We spent the afternoon talking together, the conversations conducted by gestures or routed through my American friend with his rough German. They told us how the church not only reminded them of the past but how it also was a symbol of hope for their future. They described their hopes for freedom.

The government prohibited them from talking about their faith with anyone who was not a Christian. They hoped to be free to do that without fear someday.

The government would not let them travel outside Eastern Europe, but they hoped to be free one day to come to the West. We even talked of their visiting us in the United States. Everyone smiled, but it made me sad. It seemed so hopeless a few blocks from the Berlin Wall with its concrete, barbed wire, explosives, and armed guards.

But as my East German friends hoped and dreamed— and believed— their faith helped me try to believe that it might yet be possible.

I gave my cross to the young woman who noticed it when we first met. I told her it could remind her of our shared faith. She put it on and said she would remember. I recall thinking that maybe she would come to the United States someday and give the cross back.

The Berlin Wall, the communications tower, the Iron Curtain, the Communist controls—they all cast dark shadows across Eastern European churches.

But people of faith survived.

Their hearts longed for freedom.

Their prayers cried for freedom.

Many of them died for freedom.

And somehow, some way, like the walls at Jericho, the Wall came tumbling down.

FREEDOM TODAY

Freedom is always at risk, even in America.

Governments, corporations, and institutions grow larger and more powerful. Greater wealth and influence is concentrated in fewer hands. Technology, with its potential for helping the few control the many, mutates in exponential leaps. Threats of terrorism multiply with increasingly tragic consequences. With each of these changes, our freedoms are imperiled.

> Freedom is always at risk, even in America.

As a legislator, I take an oath not to consent to "any act or thing, whatever, that shall have a tendency to lessen or abridge" the people's "rights and privileges." As a citizen, you should make a similar commitment when you vote.

Most threats to our liberties come not from outside our borders but from within. They come not from those who intentionally seek to do harm but usually from people who think they are doing good. This is true in a number of areas. One of the most publicized examples is school prayer.

SCHOOL PRAYER

All too often we hear of a student who is told he or she cannot bring a Bible to school because that would violate the separation of church and state. Or we may hear of another child instructed not to mention God in a school essay for the same reason, or of a school chorus advised not to perform a song that includes the word *God*, or of a pupil assigned to paint what she likes about spring but who is told her poster of Jesus at Easter is "too religious."

Such all-too-common incidents, reported by teachers and attorneys throughout our nation, have caused many Americans to conclude that God has been expelled from public schools. Many believe that the United States Supreme Court has ordered this expulsion and has outlawed school prayer.

Children still have the constitutional right to pray in public schools.

But, despite wide reports and common beliefs, the high court has not prohibited all voluntary prayer in public schools. Children still have the constitutional right to pray in public schools, not only silently during math tests but out loud in other situations. And children have other free speech rights, too.

Yet some teachers and administrators, like so many of us, are uncertain or misinformed about the law. They deny students their religious liberty and free speech rights. It is not that they seek to do wrong. To the contrary, they want to do right and obey the law.

Government ought not dictate our children's prayers or beliefs. But just because government should not dictate our children's prayers does not mean that government should block our children from their prayers. Government neutrality toward religion does not require government hostility to religion and religious speech.

Some people want a new amendment to the Constitution to guarantee the right to pray in schools. But what imperils our children's religious freedom is not a deficiency in the Constitution. For over two centuries, our First Amendment has served as one of the greatest protectors of freedom in human history. What imperils our children instead is the lack of understanding about our Constitution and its precepts.

The First Amendment's establishment clause does not prohibit prayer in public schools, nor has the Supreme Court ruled that it does. The First Amendment's free exercise clause protects religious liberty; its free speech provision protects religious speech. But some from both ends of the political spectrum muddy the truth, so few understand what the law says.

This is why I sponsored and the Tennessee General Assembly passed legislation to clarify the situation regarding student prayer in public schools, an example of how politics can promote and protect freedom. The bill is designed to prevent government discrimination against religion and to see that students' constitutional rights are respected. In preparing the legislation, we listened to members of diverse groups, from the Christian Coalition to Jewish Community Centers, from the American Civil Liberties Union to pastors in our districts. We worked with students, teachers, school boards, superintendents, and attorneys. Consulting the leading religious liberty lawyers and the state attorney general, we developed legislation to prevent discrimination against students of faith. While the ACLU lobbyists were not very enthusiastic, not one of these diverse groups opposed the final measure.

The legislation itself is simple, yet no other state has done so much to protect the religious freedom of its schoolchildren. The law states that public school students may voluntarily pray—silently or out loud, alone or with others—to the same extent and under the same circumstances as students are permitted to communicate nonreligious views.

If students may possess and distribute nonreligious literature, then they may have and share religious literature. If students are allowed to talk about Sammy Sosa and the Chicago Cubs during recess, they can talk about Jesus Christ and the Baptists or Abraham and the Jews or whatever their own religious beliefs may include. If students can talk to their teacher at lunch, they can also talk to God. If they can talk with one another about things secular, they can pray with one another about things sacred. If students can carry textbooks to school, they can carry Bibles, too.

The school has responsibilities to maintain order, to educate, and to protect religious minorities. Children may not infringe on a school's rights to maintain order and discipline, to prevent disruption of education, and to determine curriculum and assignments. Students may not harass others or coerce others to participate in their activities. They may not infringe on others' rights.

Some people fear that religious freedom can be abused, and clearly it can be. But we can steer wisely between extremes. We can allow students religious freedom in school without infringing on the rights of others.

We need not wait for another constitutional amendment to protect religious liberty. We just need to use the one we have.

OTHER FREEDOMS

It is not just religious freedom that is at risk today. A multitude of other freedoms are also endangered.

As an attorney, I am concerned about a freedom that underlies so many others: the right to trial by a jury of fellow citizens. Frequently today people sign dense, multipage documents with boilerplate language, required by

> It is not just religious freedom that is at risk today.

entities ranging from banks to hospitals. Few people realize that the documents often seek to take away their right to have fellow citizens hear grievances if they or their family is wronged.

As an attorney, I am also concerned that some would give government the power to lock people up without probable cause or independent judicial oversight.

As a businessman, I am concerned about undue interference by the government in my business, including the right to hire employees who share my values and religious beliefs or to contract with others who do.

As a father, I am concerned that some would take away my freedom to have my sons associate with other Boy Scouts who believe in God and who affirm the twelfth Scout law, which requires reverence.

As a sportsman, I am concerned that some would greatly restrict or even eliminate my right to take my sons hunting or sport shooting and that some read the Second Amendment as old history and not current protection.

As a citizen, I am concerned about the evaporation of our privacy. I am concerned about unreasonable searches and seizures in violation of the Fourth Amendment by governments and piracy by computer thieves and Internet predators. It is one thing for everyone in your small town to know—or think they know—most everything about you. It is another thing for your personal, medical, financial, and family data to be sucked into a giant computer system where it can be transmitted to who knows whom and be used for who knows what.

As an American, I am concerned that my family is at risk traveling overseas, simply because all Americans are potential targets of terrorists. And while we are at home, I am concerned that the often-justified fear of crime takes away our freedom to move when and where we want.

As Christians and as Americans, when we evaluate and vote on issues and candidates, freedom must be a primary concern. We should care about freedom, both at home and abroad, because God does. Political action gives us the opportunity to promote and protect freedom. Faithful politics requires nothing less.

CHAPTER 6

CHARACTERISTICS OF FAITHFUL POLITICS

*See, I am sending you out like sheep into the midst of
wolves; so be wise as serpents and innocent as doves.*
MATTHEW 10:16

*Now the works of the flesh are obvious: ... enmities, strife,
jealousy, anger, quarrels, dissensions, factions, envy,
drunkenness, carousing, and things like these. ... By
contrast, the fruit of the Spirit is love, joy, peace, patience,
kindness, generosity, faithfulness, gentleness, and self-control.*
GALATIANS 5:19-23

I've seen political friends lie, cheat, go bankrupt, steal to avoid
bankruptcy, abandon spouses, and go to prison. Friends in
politics have been arrested for tax evasion, DUI, fraud, bribery,
perjury, theft, and indecent exposure. Some have even died of
alcohol abuse, drug overdose, and suicide.

And those are just the churchgoers.

Most of these people entered politics to serve others. Many did
much good. But as the apostle Paul warned, "All have sinned and fall
short of the glory of God" (Romans 3:23).

I've also seen public servants forgo hundreds of thousands and even
millions of dollars to serve long hours for little pay at huge
sacrifices—because they wanted to serve their neighbor. They also

include many devout Christians.

Many of the finest Christians and the most devout Jews I have ever met, I came to know through politics. These public servants and private citizens are deeply committed to serving others because of their faith.

In politics, you can find both sinners and saints. You won't be able to tell them apart by how they look or which speeches they make or what party they join or which churches they attend. You can only try to tell by the way they conduct themselves, especially when no one seems to be looking. Even then, you can be sure that the most saintly still is a sinner. And the most sinful still is one for whom Christ died.

Whether more sinner or saint, a faithful politician should be committed to the *shalom* of the community he or she serves. That commitment will show itself in many specific characteristics that make up faithful politics and politicians.

"CLOTHE YOURSELVES WITH COMPASSION"[1]

The word *compassion* means "to suffer with."[2] The authors of a book titled *Compassion* write, "Compassion asks us to go where it hurts, to enter into places of pain, to share in brokenness, fear, confusion, and anguish."[3] These are not places most people, let alone politicians, want to be, yet it is where politicians must be if they are to be faithful.

Compassion is a central characteristic of God. One of the names of Christ is Immanuel, "God is with us" (Matthew 1:22-23).[4] God showed his compassion in becoming one of us, in coming to minister to the poor, sick, hungry, blind, and helpless.

Jesus shows a special concern for those in need and is repeatedly described as being moved by compassion. When Jesus saw the blind, the paralyzed, and the deaf, he experienced their pains in his own heart (see Matthew 14:14; 20:34). When Jesus saw that those who had followed him for days were tired and hungry, he was moved with compassion (see Mark 8:2). So also was he moved by the two blind men who called after him, the leper who fell to his knees in front of him, and the widow burying her only son (see Matthew 9:27; Mark 1:41; Luke 7:13).[5]

Politics provides special opportunities to share compassion with people who are poor, hungry, and powerless. Politics that is not compassionate is not faithful politics. But sometimes we politicians get so caught up in getting bills passed or our other work done that we neglect those who are suffering, the very people we are elected to serve.

Recently, my friend Michael Lamb and I were working on this book. We decided to keep working through lunch, but a man with a Vietnam Veterans baseball cap and a tattered shirt missing several buttons pulled a chair up to our table. Before I could tell him we were trying to work, he unloaded a pile of problems.

His main worry was that his wife needed health insurance.

> Politics provides special opportunities to share compassion with people who are poor, hungry, and powerless.

"Without it, she's gonna die," he said. He told us of her serious health issues in considerable detail.

My frustration at this man's interruption was finally overcome by the pathos of his desperate story. Eventually, he shook his head and looked down. "I may have to go back to Memphis to the VA [Veteran's Administration] hospital." As tears started down his cheeks, he quietly explained, "This depression." He shook his head. "Don't know if I can take any more."

His shoulders began to shake, and his face tilted toward the floor. I listened, tried to comfort him, and told him I'd try to help his wife get health insurance. "It may be an uphill struggle," I warned him, "but we'll try." He thanked me, stood slowly, and joined his wife and teenage daughter at their table.

> Faithful politics demands that we genuinely strive to understand the pain of those we serve.

Former vice president Hubert Humphrey, a man known for genuine compassion, observed that sometimes politicians fake compassion, that "in politics compassion is just part of the competition."[6] Faithful politics, however, demands that we genuinely strive to understand the pain of those we serve. It demands more than I often give. It requires that we approach others—and let ourselves be approached—with the compassion of Jesus, that we serve "with cords of human kindness, with bands of love" (Hosea 11:4).

"LOVE IS PATIENT"[7]

It is hard to be patient in politics. Everyone wants something, and they want it now. In the fast-paced, highly competitive world of politics, it is often difficult to follow the biblical injunction to "bear fruit with patient endurance" (Luke 8:15). It is even more difficult, as "the Lord's servant," to "not be quarrelsome but kindly to everyone" (2 Timothy 2:24). Quarreling is what some people assume politics is all about. Only the contentious, it seems, get what they want.

Faithful politics must operate differently.

Perhaps even more important than patience with other politicians is patience with those who need our help, being mindful of the biblical call to "encourage the faint hearted, help the weak, be patient with all of them" (1 Thessalonians 5:14).

A few hours after I listened to the veteran explain his problems during my lunch meeting, I had an opportunity to practice patience again. My twin boys had passed an important Boy Scout milestone, and we stopped on the way home for celebration milkshakes. Before I could go into McDonald's with them, a friend putting a wheelchair in a van called out my name. He wanted to talk about recent plant closings and the need for jobs. My sons came back out, and I gave them money to go get their shakes. Then a woman in the van called out. She had on huge dark glasses, and I didn't recognize her.

"Roy, this ole MS [multiple sclerosis] is getting me, but I'm a-fightin' it. I need to tell you somethin'. I've told a bunch of folks and I need to tell you."

Impatient, I wanted to join my sons inside, but instead I put my hand on her arm and forced myself to softly reply, "Well, if you've told everyone else, I'd feel left out if you didn't tell me, too."

The woman told of the difficulty of getting around town when the sidewalks are not handicapped accessible. She said she drives her motorized wheelchair in the streets, hoping not to get run over.

My boys came out again and reported that the shake machine was broken. So I sent them back to get something else, knowing going inside was not an option for me. The woman continued with stories of her struggles with the illness, weakening muscles, failing eyes. She had a story I needed to hear. Only later did I realize that this woman with the large black glasses and a face aged beyond her years was an old schoolmate.

Patience is a characteristic of faithful politics, one I often lack. Patience—as in the prayer, "Lord, I want patience and I want it *now*."

"BE QUICK TO LISTEN"[8]

The most important thing I did for the woman with MS was listen to her story. It is something Jesus did over and over. He listened to the poor, the sick, and the sinful. We are told in the book of James to "be quick to listen, slow to speak." This is hard advice for politicians who are used to others listening to them and are often taken with the sound of their own voices.

When I was first elected to the Tennessee House of Representatives, I asked the House clerk for advice. He told me, "Strap on an imaginary seat belt and keep in your seat. And don't get up to speak until you just absolutely cannot stand to be silent, and then still don't speak until you bust that seat belt."

As a part-time legislator, Roy Herron has held more than 1,000 listening meetings to hear the concerns of the citizens he represents.

The most effective public servants often are known not as much for their speaking as for their listening. My neighbor and predecessor in the House, Governor Ned McWherter, has long been known as a superb listener. Similarly, U.S. House Speaker Tip O'Neill repeatedly demanded, "Whaddaya hear?" rather than "What do you say?" and then he would listen in silence.[9]

In his book *Hardball*, Chris Matthews includes a chapter entitled "Only Talk When It Improves the Silence." He concludes that men

The most effective public servants often are known not as much for their speaking as for their listening.

and women who rise to power "succeed through a keen understanding of the institution and its members, gained not by speaking but by listening, not by barking commands but by asking the right questions."[10] Matthews recalls a leader who "listens to his colleagues with a power that most politicians cannot command at the top of their lungs."[11] I once dined with that person, and Matthews was right. Long before I read Matthews's analysis, I was impressed with how that public official listened.

In the words of a wise Southern grandmother, "God gives us two ears and but one tongue for a reason."

"CLOTHE YOURSELVES WITH . . . HUMILITY"[12]

If you do a word-association exercise with the word *politician*, you will rarely hear anyone come up with *humble*. Politicians are generally ambitious men and women who have no lack of self-confidence, and some are clearly arrogant.

The apostle Peter, however, advises us to "have unity of spirit, sympathy, love for one another, a tender heart, and a humble mind" (1 Peter 3:8). And Jesus reminds us that "all who exalt themselves will be humbled, and those who humble themselves will be exalted" (Luke 14:11).

Indeed, it is not enough to be right. What one does with the truth is as important as having the truth in the first place. And if the truth you have is only *part* of the truth, you have to be even more careful. Anyone who has had to get along with a spouse, raise children, or be on a church board knows that caution, caring, and humility are needed even (perhaps especially) when one is right. That is true in politics as well.

President Dwight D. Eisenhower said, "Humility must always be the portion of any man who receives acclaim earned in the blood of his followers and the sacrifices of his friends."[13]

In public service or when working for candidates, one must be humble enough to remember who rules in a democracy. Ultimately it is not the elected official but the people. Those too proud to remember that, those who forget whom they represent, can be reminded in even-numbered years just who is in control.

> What one does with the truth is as important as having the truth in the first place.

The famous frontiersman Davy Crockett was also Congressman Crockett. Because of his hunting exploits, tall tales, Walt Disney's movie, and our farm being near his last home, I've always been especially interested in Crockett.

Congressman Crockett's motto was, "Be always sure you're right—then go ahead."[14] That is a good motto as long as you remember how often you can be wrong.

I'm reminded of a lawyer of whom another attorney said, "I wish I was as sure about anything as he is about everything." In politics, humility helps us not claim too much, helps us listen to others, helps us be public *servants*.

"PRAY WITHOUT CEASING"[15]

Prayer helps us develop humility and practice faithful politics. Only when we make time for prayer, meditation, and reflection can we understand how best to pursue God's will and work toward *shalom*.

Too infrequently do I take time to pray. Sometimes I pray while running. The rhythm and repetition of thousands of strides and breaths helps me shed distractions and remember to whom I belong. Sometimes I meet quietly with other legislators who share my faith, if not always my party affiliation.

In *Living Faith*, President Jimmy Carter discusses how important prayer was to him when he had difficult decisions to make as president: "When I pray in such times, I try to ask myself three key questions: Are the goals that I am pursuing appropriate? Am I doing the right thing, based on my personal moral code, my Christian faith, and the duties of my current position? And, finally, have I done my best, based on the alternatives open to me? If I present all these issues to God, and then make the best possible decisions I can, things often work out well."[16]

Faithful public servants should pray and reflect to discern God's will and to make important decisions on politics and public policy. Faithful citizens should pray and reflect to discern God's will on how to evaluate, influence, and vote on politicians and public policies.

And we all should also pray for our leaders, asking, as King Solomon did, that God grant them wisdom and an "understanding mind" to lead our nation, states, counties, and communities (1 Kings 3:9). We should follow Paul's instructions in 1 Timothy 2:1-2 to offer "supplications, prayers, intercessions, and thanksgivings ... for kings and all who are in high positions, so that we may lead a quiet and peaceable life in all godliness and dignity."[17]

> Faithful citizens should pray and reflect to discern God's will on how to evaluate, influence, and vote on politicians and public policies.

Prayer is not a substitute for action. It is itself an action, one that prepares us to act wisely and faithfully in the world.

"LOVE YOUR ENEMIES"[18]

In the heat of partisan debate, it is easy to see political opponents only as enemies, not as brothers and sisters whom God loves. And loving our enemies, especially our political enemies, is often the last thing we feel like doing. It is right to be passionate and committed in politics, but there is no room in faithful politics for the anger, resentment, and revenge that characterize so much of contemporary political life.

Jesus calls us to love our neighbors as ourselves, even the neighbors who disagree or attack us. In his Sermon on the Mount, Jesus teaches: "Love your enemies, do good to those who hate you, bless those who curse you, pray for those who abuse you" (Luke 6:27-28).

> It is right to be passionate and committed in politics, but there is no room in faithful politics for anger, resentment, and revenge.

It is difficult, if not impossible, to love our enemies without forgiving them. Since politics is often a competitive "zero-sum game" in which one person or group wins and another loses, revenge is a frequent temptation. It is hard to forgive those who attack us with negative statements or false ads, criticize our character and commitments, or use every possible means to defeat or sabotage our efforts to do what we think is right.

Once when I ran for the legislature, my opponent was a friend and former supporter. His campaign, however, focused on attacking me. I prayed constantly for grace to love.

Turning the other cheek, as Jesus instructs in Matthew 5:39, was almost more than I could do—and it is more than I have done on many occasions. Still, Jesus reminds us that our own forgiveness is tied to our willingness to forgive: "Forgive, and you will be forgiven" (Luke 6:37).

After that election, eventually my friendship with my opponent was renewed. I think of him as a friend and a brother in Christ.

Are Jesus' commands unrealistic for rough-and-tumble modern politics? Some think that religion, as well as values originating in religion, should be kept totally out of politics. Others think there is a place for these values but not at the cost of winning elections and defeating enemies.

But if there is no place for these high biblical standards in politics, then there is no place for them anywhere else in our lives either. We have to believe that God wants love, including love of enemies, to characterize our politics as well as our homes and churches.

Within the last two weeks at the Capitol, I have lined up with a Republican colleague on one issue against a Democrat, then turned around on another issue to work with the Democrat against the Republican. Yesterday, I was on the floor of the Senate, working with the Republican against the Democrat.

Politics should be about issues, not personalities or parties. Legislating should be about what is right, not whom you're mad at.

That is possible only if one can love one's enemies. It is easier if one remembers that today's foe may need to be tomorrow's friend.

"SPEAKING THE TRUTH IN LOVE"[19]

John says Jesus was "full of grace and truth" (John 1:14). John's Gospel also tells us, "You will know the truth, and the truth will make you free" (8:32); God must be worshipped "in spirit and truth" (4:24); God will send us "the Spirit of truth" (14:17); and God will "sanctify [us] in the truth; [his] word is truth" (17:17).

The apostle Paul also emphasizes the importance of truthfulness, telling the church at Rome, "I am speaking the truth in Christ—I am not lying." Paul denounces the wicked who "suppress the truth" (Romans 9:1; 1:18). To the church at Corinth, Paul says that love "rejoices in the truth," and he later writes, "We cannot do anything against the truth, but only for the truth" (1 Corinthians 13:6; 2 Corinthians 13:8).

To the church at Ephesus, Paul stresses "speaking the *truth* in love," "speak[ing] the *truth* to our neighbors," and he urges the people to "fasten the belt of *truth* around your waist" (Ephesians 4:15; 4:25; 6:14, italics added).

Whatever else Christians are to do, we are to tell the truth.

And yet, when I ask people to describe politicians in one word, they often reply *dishonest* or *lying*. I have yet to hear someone say with a straight face *honest* or *truthful*. If people will talk this way to an elected official's face, imagine how little they really think of politicians' honesty.

Sadly, people have reasons to think politicians are dishonest, rarely telling the truth. Most politicians who get into trouble do so because they want something else too much or truth too little. President Nixon's downfall came not because of the Watergate burglary, but because he lied about it. President Clinton's troubles over his adultery escalated to another level when it was revealed that he lied.

On the other hand, Senator Robert Taft of Ohio was described as "born to integrity."[20] President John F. Kennedy wrote that Taft was "known in the Senate as a man who never broke an agreement, who never compromised his deeply felt Republican principles, who never practiced political deception."[21] Even Taft's bitter political foe, President Harry Truman, said this at Taft's death: "He and I did not agree on public policy, but ... we need intellectually honest men like Senator Taft."[22]

Today, much of Senator John McCain's national, bipartisan appeal is that people believe he is speaking truthfully and from the heart. Now, perhaps more than ever, we need leaders, followers, and all citizens willing to "speak the truth in love."

People get mad at officeholders when they feel the lawmaker is not honest with them. But constituents usually understand if they see an issue differently than the officeholder, at least if the officeholder tells them the truth in love.

Similarly, leaders can hear citizens best if the citizens do not speak hatefully but rather truthfully with love.

"TAKE COURAGE"[23]

Telling the truth is often not possible without another biblical virtue: courage. It is easy to tell the truth, show compassion for the poor, or love your enemy when everyone will praise you for it. But when doing right will only draw heated opposition, you need courage. Stephen Carter recognizes the connection between courage and integrity and argues that "*saying openly* that you are acting on your understanding of right and wrong" is one criterion of integrity.[24]

> Telling the truth is often not possible without another biblical virtue: courage.

Praise of courage runs throughout the Bible. In Chronicles, for example, we see the refrain, "Be strong and of good courage" (1 Chronicles 22:13; 2 Chronicles 32:7). We read repeatedly the admonitions to "take courage" or "keep up your courage" throughout the Bible. These are just a few examples: 2 Chronicles 15:7; Ezra 7:28; Psalm 31:24; Isaiah 41:6; Haggai 2:4; John 16:33; Acts 23:11; 27:22, 25; and 1 Thessalonians 2:2.

The Scriptures are full of stories of great courage, from David facing Goliath, to Queen Esther risking death, to Jesus facing the Cross.

Where do we see courage in politics?

Perhaps the most famous collection of American stories of political courage is President John F. Kennedy's *Profiles in Courage*. The book tells the stories of eight United States senators who exhibited extraordinary courage in times of great moral crisis. But political courage is not just historical.

During the last legislative session, I saw a colleague exhibit such extraordinary courage.

Tennessee senator Charlotte Burks is the widow of a state senator. Her late husband, Senator Tommy Burks, was murdered by his political opponent. She succeeded her husband to the same office.

Senator Burks has continued to represent the views and values she and her late husband share with her district. Among those values is a commitment to protect the unborn. She is unashamedly pro-life.

Recently, legislation was on the floor of the Tennessee Senate that would have begun the process of amending our state constitution. The amendment would have removed any state constitutional right to an abortion. Senator Burks supported the legislation. She wanted, however, to let women whose lives were truly endangered by pregnancy be able to decide whether they could save their own lives. She also thought that government should not interfere in the decision of the family of a child rape victim to end that pregnancy, and she believed that victims of rape and incest should not be forced by the government to bear the rapists' children.

When the pro-life Senator Burks sponsored an amendment to protect these girls and women—and also to constitutionally ban partial-birth abortion— some attacked her politically. Flyers were handed out in her district. And then came the death threat.

An anonymous male called Senator Burks' office and snarled, "I'm going to kill the baby killer!"

Can you imagine such a threat against a woman whose husband had been murdered by a political opponent a few short years earlier? Can you imagine how she and her daughters felt?

But in the face of numerous political threats and even this death threat, Senator Burks refused to bow. In fact, any chance this devout and courageous Christian would change her mind ended with that threat to her life.

Senator Burks is a woman of deep faith who bears constant witness to her Lord. One of the many ways she bears witness is with the courage of her convictions. Extraordinary and faithful courage.

President Andrew Jackson said, "One man with courage makes a majority."[25] So does one woman.

"THE FRUIT OF THE SPIRIT IS ... JOY"[26]

James tells us, "My brothers and sisters, whenever you face trials of any kind, consider it nothing but joy" (James 1:2). Indeed, as Christians we should be "filled with joy and with the Holy Spirit" (Acts 13:52).

But joy is one characteristic that citizens often do not see in their public officials, even those who are Christians. Perhaps some people distrust Christians in politics not only because they lack joy but also because they are angry. Stephen Carter writes, "Although the religious voice belongs in American politics, it will be an ineffective and scary voice as long as it seems to be a mean-spirited voice."[27]

Indeed, in the heat of partisan debate, it is easy to become angry. But as Christians, we are called to be "slow to anger; for [our] anger does not produce God's righteousness" (James 1:19-20).

Laughter helps us be slow to anger and renews our joy.

As the Grand Ole Opry star Minnie Pearl used to say, "Laughter is God's hand on the shoulder of a troubled world." After serving in government, wrestling with some of the problems of this troubled world, I know what a blessing laughter can be.

Laughter helps us avoid taking ourselves too seriously. G. K. Chesterton opined that "angels can fly because they take themselves lightly."[28] If people in politics hope to soar or at least get airborne, we have to take ourselves lightly, too. The challenge is to take our calling seriously but ourselves lightly.

The Christian humorist Grady Nutt reminded people not to take themselves too seriously: "If you don't think God is a humorist, you need to look in the mirror every now and then." Tennessee humorist and politician L. H. "Cotton" Ivy adds, "If after looking in the mirror you still cannot laugh, then at least you will know what everyone else is laughing at."[29]

How can Christians do politics? Only by the grace of God and with a sense of humor. Often with jokes, occasionally with pranks, frequently by seeing the humor in humanity, not infrequently by revealing our own funny flaws. This is how we can give joy and have joy.

My mother used to tell me, "Sometimes you have to laugh to keep from crying." It is especially true for politicians and other people in public life. When the issues are hard, the hours are long, and the public pressure is stressful, joy and humor can be the salves that ease tensions and the grease that keeps the cogs of government moving. Most importantly, joy witnesses to the abundant grace of God.

If we really know how tough things are for some people, at times we are sad. But if we remember how good God has been to us, we have many reasons to be joyful. And that joy lifts us and helps us address people's problems and serve those in need.

Compassion, patience, listening, humility, prayer, love, truth, courage, joy. How many people associate any of these words with politics? How many associate them with Christian politicians? And yet these are exactly what should characterize anything that we dare to call faithful politics.

CHAPTER 7

BEYOND PARTISANSHIP: SERVING GOD, NOT IDEOLOGY

I appeal to you therefore, brothers and sisters, by the mercies of God, to present your bodies as a living sacrifice, holy and acceptable to God, which is your spiritual worship. Do not be conformed to this world, but be transformed by the renewing of your minds, so that you may discern what is the will of God—what is good and acceptable and perfect.
ROMANS 12:1-2

We are called to be people of conviction, not conformity; of moral nobility, not social respectability. We are commanded to live differently and according to a higher loyalty.
DR. MARTIN LUTHER KING, JR.

This country needs far less partisanship and much more patriotism, less enmity and more comity, less yelling at or about the other party and more listening to and learning from the other party.

No party has a monopoly on judgment or truth. We often learn the most from opponents during elections and debates. And that is the strength and beauty of America, of democracy, of God's world. I have heard people ask, "How can someone be a Christian and a Democrat?"

I have heard others ask, "How can someone be a Christian and a Republican?" Frankly, I think it makes more sense to be a Christian and either a Democrat or a Republican than to be a Christian and have no interest in political and social issues at all.

Is God a Republican? Is God a Democrat? You would think God was one or the other, given how many people claim God is on their side. Furthermore, many are sure God hates the same people they hate. If you find yourself thinking that way, consider Anne Lamott's observation that "you can safely assume you've created God in your own image when it turns out that God hates all the same people you do."[1]

It is safe to say that God is not greatly impressed with either Republicans or Democrats. God is not on the side of any political party but on the side of justice, compassion, truth, mercy, freedom, and life. I am reminded of what Abraham Lincoln said when he overheard a clergyman say he hoped "the Lord is on our side." Lincoln responded, "I know that the Lord is always on the side of the right. But it is my constant anxiety and prayer that this nation should be on the Lord's side."[2] That should also be our prayer.

> God is not on the side of any political party but on the side of justice, compassion, truth, mercy, freedom, and life.

Christians too often put their hopes in political parties and ideologies. In the 1960s and 1970s, issues of social justice, like civil rights, hungry children, and the Vietnam War, were at the forefront in many churches. Some Christians looked to liberal politics to speak the truth of God to society.

In the 1980s and 1990s, issues relating to sexual morality, including abortion, promiscuity, and homosexuality, were at the forefront in many churches. Some Christians thought conservative politics was the key to redeeming society.

Politics didn't save us in the last century, and it won't save us in this one. But that does not mean we should not be involved in politics. Believers are called into the political arena as in every other area of life. We should not just *be* there, we should be committed and passionate. But our commitment should ultimately be to something much higher than political party or ideology.

HEALTHY AND UNHEALTHY COMPROMISE

When I ask Christians, "Why don't you want to be involved in politics?" many respond that they do not want to "compromise their principles" or "dirty their hands." Indeed, many assume a Christian cannot enter politics without compromising beliefs or integrity.

I agree that compromise, in the sense of abandoning core values, is a real danger. But I also know that another notion of compromise, the act of settling for less than everything one wants, is necessary not only in politics but in all of life in a fallen world.

> Our country as we know it would not exist without compromise.

Indeed, our country as we know it would not exist without compromise. Compromise has characterized the American political system since the birth of our nation. During the Constitutional Convention of 1787, our nation's founders were forced to compromise in order to establish a system that satisfied the interests of states large and small, Northern and Southern. Without compromise, the convention would have dissolved, and the great experiment of American democracy would have failed from the start.

Whether or not we like it, compromise in politics is a necessity, even a moral good. It is necessary both because of our finiteness and because we live in community with others. "Democracy," writes Richard John Neuhaus, "is the product not of a vision of perfection but of the knowledge of imperfection. In this view, compromise is not an immoral act, nor is it an amoral act. That is, the one who compromises does not step out of her role as a moral actor. To the contrary, the person who makes a compromise is making a moral judgment about what is to be done when moral judgments are in conflict."[3]

COMPROMISE AND INTEGRITY

Faithful Christians and unbridled idealists often suggest that compromise—settling for anything less than the complete victory of their values and vision—destroys integrity. Compromise, however, is compatible with integrity, perhaps even necessary to preserve integrity.

A central part of the definition of integrity is wholeness. As Stephen Carter points out, the Latin root for *integrity* is the same as that of *integer*, a whole number. "A person of integrity, like a whole number, is a whole person, a person somehow undivided."[4] In a person of integrity, all aspects are integrated, working together to achieve the ultimate purpose of that person.

> Compromise is compatible with integrity, perhaps even necessary to preserve integrity.

For people of faith, the concepts of wholeness and integration are familiar ones. As we have seen, in the Bible these ideas are expressed in the concept of *shalom*. God calls us to have integrity and seek peace and wholeness in our religious, political, economic, social, and individual lives and relationships.

If we remember this idea of wholeness, it is only by compromising at times that we can live with peace and integrity. If we insist uncompromisingly on having our way, we will fuel opposition and fracture the peace of *shalom*. One might argue that if the price of truth is war, then war it should be. But this ignores the fact that our own understanding of the truth is always partial and flawed. If we really love the truth, we will work to get as much of it into the world as possible, and that may require settling for less than the ideal.

Sometimes the question is whether we want the world to be a better place, even if only somewhat better, more than we want to win. Uncompromising politics and politicians often are ineffective. They do not bring more truth and goodness into the everyday world because they are not willing to work with anyone who sees things differently than they do.

Further, if they believe that change can and must come overnight, they are often not only ineffective but also disappointed. Most often, positive change only comes gradually, in small increments, with sustained effort, commitment, and yes, compromise.

> Most often, positive change only comes gradually and with compromise.

Politicians are not the only people who recognize the need for compromise. Even the pope compromises on occasion. In his *Evangelium Vitae* (*The Gospel of Life*, 1995), Pope John Paul II advised pro-life politicians to support legislation that reduces the number of abortions but does not ban abortion, even though the Catholic church strongly opposes the practice of abortion.[5]

"In this," observes Stephen Carter, "the pope is acknowledging human reality: rarely can any of us achieve our moral ends perfectly, or all at once. Integrity will at times require that we take what we can get."[6] Indeed, positive change, however small, is better than no change at all.

But while Christian politicians must compromise if they are to help improve the real world, they must not be conformed to the world. As John F. Kennedy wrote, "We shall need compromises in the days ahead, to be sure. But these will be, or should be, compromises of issues, not principles. We can compromise our political positions, but we cannot compromise ourselves. We can resolve the clash of interests without conceding our ideals."[7]

Christians must compromise, but only when that compromise produces some movement toward, not away from, a goal or end that is right and good.[8] Compromise should be the means to an end but not an end in itself. "A temporary compromise is a diplomatic act," writes Leon Stein, "but a permanent compromise is the abandonment of a goal."[9] Christians sometimes must compromise in order to bring more light into the world, but they can and must do so in service to the God who is the source of all light.

> Christians sometimes must compromise in order to bring more light into the world.

A QUESTIONABLE COMPROMISE

Being a legislator brings pressure to conform to this world. One day early in my legislative tenure, I felt so much pressure to conform that I wrote down what had happened; I wanted to confess my sins to a church I was invited to preach at. It was definitely a sermon more for this preacher than the congregation.

That week I had voted on a bill to let judges establish work-release programs for certain prisoners in limited circumstances. I initially pushed the green button to vote for the bill, but when I saw it was going to lose—there were so many red lights on the voting board—I thought, *Why should I give an opponent an issue to distort against me next year when an "aye" vote will do no one any good?*

And I thought about the questions of a senior member of the legislature whom I respect: "What happens if the local sheriff does not want a work-release program? Could the judges set it up anyway?" They could under that bill.

So when the Speaker asked before he closed voting, "Does anyone wish to change their vote?" I pushed the red button and voted no. The bill was defeated by a substantial margin.

Was I one of those whom H. L. Mencken described as having "compromised with their honor ... by swallowing their convictions"?[10] Was I one of those President Lincoln described as having "interests aside from the interests of the people" or "at least one step removed from honest"?[11]

Was I no better than what Walter Lippmann described politicians to be—"insecure and intimidated men"?[12]

And most importantly, was I acting against the apostle Paul's counsel not to conform to this world?

A HEALTHY COMPROMISE

If I blew it on the work-release vote, I hope I have more often compromised in a healthy way as a Christian and a politician.

Early in my legislative service, I learned of senior citizens being deceived by unscrupulous sellers of Medigap insurance. These insurance policies were supposed to pay for medical expenses not covered by Medicare. Unfortunately, however, too often the policies cost a lot and covered little.

Just as bad or worse, agents who received much larger commissions for selling a new policy than for renewing an existing one would "flip" seniors from company to company so they could receive larger fees. The poor seniors, however, would be excluded from coverage for preexisting conditions for a year after they bought the new policies. Of course, for many seniors, almost everything was deemed a preexisting condition. Since the agents were flipping them from company to company so often, the seniors were purchasing insurance that frequently did them no good at all.

> I hope I have more often compromised in a healthy way as a Christian and a politician.

The Medigap industry and I fought over the shape of the legislation needed to put a stop to these practices. But I slowly discovered responsible leaders in the industry who also abhorred the abuses.

After many meetings, we found a way to protect seniors without making it impossible for responsible companies to serve them. We crafted a win-win solution.

I remember the day we found that solution and how surprised I was. I recall thinking how important it was to keep talking and, especially, listening so that a workable consensus could come about.

This type of legislating and policy making is not compromise in a weak, morally deficient way. Instead, it is consensus building in a peacemaking way.

As Jim Wallis points out, "Building consensus, creating common ground, and finding workable solutions to intractable problems are far more difficult tasks than endless ideological posturing and partisan attacking."[13]

COMPROMISING CITIZENS

I have focused on the need for politicians to compromise without conforming. Christian citizens have a similar responsibility when trying to determine which candidate to support in a campaign.

> To be silent and refuse to support one candidate out of fear of compromise would be to abandon our responsibility.

There is seldom a candidate who agrees with your position on every political issue. You may agree with one candidate on one issue and the opposing candidate on another. In such a situation, supporting either candidate requires you to compromise to some extent. But should you avoid supporting candidates and voting because you are afraid you will compromise your integrity or faith?

Absolutely not. Christians need a voice in the political process. To be silent and refuse to support one candidate out of fear of compromise would be to abandon our responsibility to be involved in shaping our society. There is rarely a perfect candidate, just as there is rarely a perfect bill. We need to acknowledge this reality and vote in the ways that best advance our vision and values, even if such action demands compromise.

HEALTHY PARTISANSHIP?

In my father's day, your political party often was determined by where you were born. For the most part, if you were raised in the rural South, you were a Democrat. In the Depression my grandparents almost lost their farm because they could not get enough money for their crops in order to pay the taxes. My father, thanks to a Democratic judge, had a clerk's job in the courthouse and therefore had a salary. He had to pay his parents' taxes. Then came the New Deal, and farmers had a prayer—and decent prices for their crops.

Dad was, I have always been told, the youngest delegate to the Democratic National Convention in 1936.

My great-uncle Dean was a Democratic state representative and senator in the 1940s and 1950s.

Uncle Dean and my grandfather both served as members of the Weakley County Court for more than three decades. Other relatives were sheriffs. All were Democrats, of course.

In 1967, Dad had a heart attack. A Democratic Speaker of the House got a Democratic governor to appoint him to a judgeship, where less stress enabled Dad to live—and serve—another nine years.

In fact, partisan considerations seemed even to enter into our family's courting. When my older brother Dean wanted to get married, he had to bring his prospective bride home to Weakley County to meet Mammy, the family matriarch.

If by partisanship you mean commitment to a set of principles and values, and the determination to work to see them find expression in the real world, then I am all for it.

"Lean over, child," the ancient woman said from her bed to my future sister-in-law. Diane leaned down so the lamplight hit her face. Mammy touched her cheek gently with gnarled old fingers.

"I have but one question, my child," Mammy whispered. "Are you a Democrat or a Republican?"

Diane, being well prepared, quickly replied, "A Democrat."

Mammy patted Diane's cheek and smiled. "Then you have my blessing," she said.

112

Friends who grew up in Republican areas had similar experiences and allegiances to the Republican Party.

For decades, that's the way it was. People were partisan and did not apologize for it. And for many today it is still that way.

Is partisanship good? It depends on what you mean by the word *partisanship*.

If you mean unthinking allegiance to a political party or ideology, then I am against it. If you mean a willingness to do anything, including distort and lie, to defeat one's enemies and achieve political ends, then I am against it. If you mean an unwillingness to listen or learn from those not expressing exactly your beliefs in exactly your way, then I am definitely against it.

But if by *partisanship* you mean commitment to a set of principles and values, and the determination to work to see them find expression in the real world, then I am all for partisanship. And I am all for joining one party or the other (or a third) and doing what you can to see that your party genuinely defends and embodies those values.

When we do that, we are demanding the best of our political party and politicians, rather than simply trying to win elections and hold power. And when we recognize that no party or ideology holds all God's truth, then we may even be willing to compromise.

THE PARABLE OF THE GOOD REPUBLICAN

When Jesus told the parable of the Good Samaritan, he was, among other things, trying to get his Jewish listeners to put together, for perhaps the first time in their lives, the words *good* and *Samaritan*. It is a story that should prompt us to rethink who is good and who is not, and who our enemies are.

I have a story from my own family that parallels the story of the Good Samaritan, and it teaches something about compromise and learning from one's supposed enemies.

My sister, Betsye, is older than I am. At nineteen, a bright and beautiful young woman, she married. The homecoming queen married the football player from a nearby town, who soon would be flying air force jets.

The marriage of the dream couple eventually turned into a nightmare. Betsye hung in there as long as she could, but before long they were divorced.

Betsye finished college, started teaching, and found another fellow. He was the son of a lawyer, from a good Democratic family, and they married. Betsye put him through law school, bore him a handsome son, then watched him move out. They, too, divorced.

These two unhappy marriages and divorces stripped my sister of self-confidence and self-esteem. Her once bright future had become an all too painful present.

MEETING CHARLIE

One weekend I came home from law school, and Mother told me that Betsye wanted us to come to her place for dinner. She wanted us to meet someone.

I was decidedly unenthused as we sat waiting for him. I did not know much about this fellow. I had been told that he was a doctor—that sounded good.

But I also learned that he had been a delegate to a Republican National Convention—that sounded bad.

His dad was a Baptist preacher—that could be either good or bad.

He was going to cook supper for us—I would wait to see if that was good or bad. I didn't have to wait long.

"Hello, Roy," he said when he arrived. "I'm Charlie Hickman."

He obviously was much too old for my sister. As I shook his hand, however, I discovered the old geezer had a good grip. I tried not to show the pain as I pulled back my hurting hand.

"You go to Vanderbilt Law School?" he asked.

I acknowledged that I did.

"Isn't that where that [string of expletives] Albert Gore teaches?"

"No, no sir," I stammered, a bit taken aback by both the language and the venom.

"I don't mean that no-count young one, but the old man. Doesn't that [expletive] teach there?"

"No. No sir," I replied.

Mother had warned me not to talk politics. Apparently they had not warned Charlie, because before long he was telling me that he was a delegate for Senator Barry Goldwater at the 1964 Republican National Convention.

So much for avoiding politics.

We went into the living room and sat down to visit. He launched into telling jokes. I tried to laugh. Until he told a racist joke. As it started, I looked down at the floor. I did not look up when he finished but excused myself and went to another room.

In the kitchen, as Betsye and Charlie fixed our supper, he wanted to talk about sports. Good.

He was an Ole Miss football fan and they had beaten my University of Tennessee Volunteers that year. Bad.

So much for sports.

Charlie smoked like a chimney. My contact lenses became dry, and my eyes were burning. My eyes were not the only part of me that was suffering.

By dinner I was saying nothing. I was eyeing the door, thinking Charlie had offended me and disagreed with me in every way possible.

Wrong.

Over the steaks, Charlie wanted to talk religion. He inquired about my being in divinity school. I reluctantly admitted that I was. He proceeded to tell me about Hal Lindsey and his book *The Late Great Planet Earth*. Never mind that I had already read it. He proceeded to tell me that Lindsey was right, that the world was about to end. Furthermore, it would end during our lifetimes.

If that were right, I silently thought, *could it please be soon—like before Charlie opens his mouth again?*

Eventually, the evening ended, even if the world did not. Mom and I started home.

Mother waited until we were almost out of the driveway before asking, "Well, how did you like Charlie?"

I did not tell her that except for his politics, religion, racism, football team, smoking, cursing, and being too old for my sister, he seemed okay.

Instead, dutiful son that I am, I tried not to tell the truth without telling a lie. "Well, Mom, he seems real interesting," I replied. "What did you think?"

Mother said she thought he was real nice.

I think my own mother lied to me.

THE MARRIAGE

A few weeks later, Charlie's Baptist preacher father and I performed the wedding.

I was sure Betsye was marrying too soon—and the wrong man. But she had already made the decision.

Let me tell you about this Republican rascal she married.

He took her eight-year-old son and made him his own. He fixed a desk and a bookshelf in his new son's room. He colored and painted with him. Fixed model airplanes and ships. Worked math problems. Spelled words. Saw that he wanted for nothing. Did everything he knew to do to earn his respect, to gain his love. He did all anyone could do for that boy. And then he did more.

He bought him a car when the time came (even before the time came). He took that little boy to cities and ball games (admittedly, mostly to Ole Miss games). He raised him as his own. That little boy who had so needed a father at home healed and grew and became a courteous, compassionate, wonderful man.

And what about my sister Betsye?

After they married, Betsye did not fix dinner again for years. Charlie always cooked. He would get home from work and cook for her, wait on her, and insist that he enjoyed it. He did enjoy it. And so did she.

He built her a new home—their home.

He took her to New Orleans, to his favorite restaurants, and anywhere else she wanted to go. He courted her, his wife, like they were young and he wanted her to want to go out with him again. He loved her every single way he knew how.

And my sister—whose confidence and self-esteem had almost evaporated—my sister came back.

Charlie treated her like the lovely, laughing, loving person that he knew she could be. And she became that person again.

The physician healed her.

LIVING OUT GALATIANS 3:28

By the side of the road the "Good Republican" found an injured woman and a wounded young boy. And he took care of them.

The wounded were healed. The hurting were made whole. And I was astonished.

What Democrat would have thought that a Republican, especially this one, would be the Good Samaritan?

Any way that you and I can divide us up, God can put us together.

By the side of the road the "Good Republican" found an injured woman and a wounded young boy. And he took care of them.

Whoever we categorize and put in a box, God can free. And the good news is this: As that person is freed from our stereotypes and prejudices, we are freed also.

To paraphrase the apostle Paul:

> For we are neither Jew nor Greek, nor Samaritan, neither slave nor free, neither male nor female, neither Democrat nor Republican; but we are all one in God's love.

Thanks be to God.

Thanks be to God for our neighbors.

All of them.

CHAPTER 8

EVALUATING POLITICIANS AND POLICIES

*Do nothing from selfishness or conceit, but in humility
count others better than yourselves. Let each of you look not
only to his own interests, but also to the interests of others.*
PHILIPPIANS 2:3-4, RSV

As Flannery O'Connor wrote, "A good man is hard to find"—
and so is a good woman. If this saying is valid in general, it is
especially true when looking for political candidates we can support
enthusiastically. How do we wade through the blizzard of claims and
counterclaims—most designed to persuade, not inform—to discern
who has the wisdom, values, and insight necessary to lead us? Is it
enough that a candidate shares our religious convictions? Or belongs
to our political party? Or is successful, rich, and even good-looking?

In addition to candidates, there are many, many political proposals
and positions to evaluate. Most are couched in attractive or hot-
button terms, purportedly good for us and for society. How can we
know which policies to support and which to oppose?

We should evaluate politicians the same way we choose friends or
spouses—by evaluating their character. And when evaluating policies
and proposals, we should ask the recurring question in this book:
Does it contribute to *shalom*?

EVALUATING CANDIDATES

What should Christians look for in political candidates?

In chapter 6, we discussed some of the key characteristics of faithful politics. Those characteristics, of course, should also be ones we look for in a faithful politician.

CHARACTER

Nothing is more important than that a candidate be a person of character. Character is values in action, and it defines who we are more than any other measure. A faithful candidate is committed to the biblical concepts that we have already discussed—justice, freedom, compassion, and life. But it is not enough simply to *say* that one is for these things. Candidates must practically demonstrate their commitment by their political records or by a detailed indication of what policies and practices they will support.

Justice, compassion, and freedom do not thrive in the world by wishing. They are the product of endless personal and collective choices. Choices define character. We should not support a candidate until we have investigated the choices—personal and political—that candidate has made. Similarly, a politician who gives platitudinous or evasive answers to important questions is not likely to possess the kind of character necessary for leadership.

We should try to discern a person's motive in running for office. Is it to do justice and to protect freedom, or is it just to gain power and stature? How do his positions on the issues align with these concepts? What issues does she care most about? Does he have a history of service in his private and public life, or is political office simply another way of achieving individual success?

> We should not support a candidate until we have investigated the choices—personal and political—that candidate has made.

A faithful candidate does more than speak the language of faith. Often on the campaign trail, we hear candidates who explicitly express their faith or engage in what some describe as "God-talk."[2] I want to hear how a candidate's faith affects the person he is and the positions he takes on certain issues. But sometimes politicians just want to let you know they share your religious faith without describing how their faith influences their leadership or their politics. We must choose political leaders who not only make testimonies of faith but are committed to living their faith through action, especially political action.

As Americans, we depend on our elected representatives to make important, sometimes even life and death decisions. Therefore, we want to put our lives and livelihoods in the hands of leaders we trust, leaders who are honest, contemplative, open-minded, courageous, and compassionate.

Basic honesty, as we have discussed, is a bedrock requirement for faithful politics and politicians. Honesty by itself, however, is not enough. As Stephen Carter points out, telling the truth requires knowing what the truth is: "A person may be entirely honest without ever engaging in the hard work of discernment that integrity requires; she may tell us quite truthfully what she believes without ever taking the time to figure out whether what she believes is good and right and true."[3]

All candidates, for instance, will say they are for compassion. But do the policies they support coincide with a biblical understanding of compassion? Would Jesus recognize their choices as compassionate choices?

The fact is, many times it is difficult to know what the compassionate or just choice is in politics. It is often not a clear question of good versus evil or light versus darkness. Politicians and lobbyists excel at making even bad bills sound good. It often takes hard work, thoughtfulness, and honesty to arrive at the kind of wisdom we call discernment. Consider which candidates are willing to seek the truth, to understand the complexities and nuances of issues, to put in the time and effort to think through proposals and policies before stating their opinion.

OPEN-MINDEDNESS AND HUMILITY

Discernment is closely related to two other qualities we should seek in candidates. Those who truly are attempting to discern what is right are committing themselves to open-mindedness and humility. They are saying, "I do not yet possess the entire truth on this. I need to know more." They must be willing to forsake preconceived notions and automatic loyalty to party or ideology.

Too often we mistake arrogance for conviction. The politician who speaks with complete confidence, belittles those who see things differently, and never expresses any sense of how difficult it is sometimes to know what's best is more arrogant than wise. These are not the qualities of the great leaders in the Bible, nor are they qualities we should accept in our politicians.

> Too often we mistake arrogance for conviction.

COURAGE

The ancients recognized that right thinking is ineffectual without right acting, and that acting often requires courage. Some leaders, whether in politics or in the church, are wonderful people, full of wisdom and compassion, but do not possess the courage to stand up for what they believe. We need political leaders who, after contemplation and reflection on an issue, have the courage to act in the face of opposition.

COMPASSION

As we have seen, we also need to consider whether candidates embody the compassion we should expect of those whose call is to serve others. Jesus called each of us to reach out to others in love and to help those in need.

Ask yourself whether a candidate will be committed to serving others while in office. Will that candidate respond to the needs of the community and the nation in a compassionate way?

INTELLIGENCE AND ABILITY

We need candidates who not only have the moral character to lead but who also are equipped with the political knowledge and skill to be effective.

Finally, we must also look at a candidate's intelligence and experience. A candidate may be the most upright citizen and Christian that we know but may not know anything about government, politics, or public policy. We need candidates who not only have the moral character to lead but who also are equipped with the political knowledge and skill to be effective.

FINDING OUT WHAT WE NEED TO KNOW

How do we go about determining a candidate's character, intelligence, or political experience?

We can find out about candidates in several ways.

First, talk to the candidates or hear what the candidates have to say. Attend rallies, political fundraisers, or campaign events. Listen to speeches or debates. Ask candidates about specific issues, bills, or proposals. Determine candidates' positions on the issues you care most about.[4]

Second, look at how the candidates are running their campaigns. Are they willing to debate and talk about the issues? Do their ads describe their positions on issues or merely portray images and make emotional appeals? What do campaign materials (direct-mail letters, campaign brochures, websites, e-mails) reveal about the candidates?[5]

Investigate which individuals or political action committees (PACs) are contributing to the campaign. You can do this by checking with the local or federal election finance commissions or by reading newspaper articles that discuss campaign finance.[6]

Next, learn about the candidate's previous experience in similar positions of leadership. Did the person act with integrity? What is the candidate's voting record on the issues you care most about? What is his or her knowledge about the issues and the community? What are the candidate's accomplishments or failures in positions of leadership? Has he or she shown the qualities of a political leader or potential political leader?

Find out about the candidate's party affiliation and the party's platform. What positions on the issues does that party promote? How tied is the candidate to party loyalty?

Then find out what other people have to say about the candidate. Call the candidate's campaign or political party headquarters. Read articles, profiles, or press reports about the person. Talk to local reporters, political science professors, volunteers, or other community leaders who can tell you about the candidate. Find out who has endorsed the candidate by calling the campaign headquarters or by looking at the ratings that different interest groups have given the candidate. These endorsements and interest group ratings may reveal the candidate's priorities on the issues. Talk to people who know the person well—friends, colleagues, staffers, or volunteers. Find out what has shaped their views of the candidate and why they support or oppose the candidate.[7]

Some groups, such as the League of Women Voters, recommend preparing a "candidate report card," giving the candidates grades according to how they stand on certain issues that are important to the voter; their background, experience, and leadership qualities; and how fairly and honestly they have run their campaign.[8] Other people may want to arrange a discussion group with friends and family to discuss different candidates and issues and to share the results of each other's investigations.

Taking the time to learn about candidates to make informed decisions matters. After all, the quality of American democracy depends on the quality of our votes.

EVALUATING POLICIES AND PROPOSALS

During the most recent legislative session, my legislative intern asked me, "How do you decide how to vote on an issue?"[9]

Determining my stance on an issue is challenging at times, especially when I am trying to determine a Christian position on an issue, something that must be pursued vigorously but proclaimed cautiously.

Determining a Christian position on an issue must be approached with the utmost humility. Especially when we are trying to discern the will of God in a democracy, we cannot, we must not, claim too much. We must always consider that we might be wrong or that, at the very least, the issue might have complexities not yet known.

Different communities of faith approach discerning God's will about public policy issues in different ways. As a Methodist, I find John Wesley's quadrilateral approach helpful.[10] That requires looking first to Scripture. What, if anything, does the Bible say about this issue?

Second, we look to tradition. What are the historical teachings of the church on this issue?

Third, we look to experience. What do our own experiences and the experiences of others tell us about this issue?

Finally, we look to reason. Does it make sense? What are the consequences (intended or not) of the proposed action?

Taken together, with the Bible at the helm, Wesley's fourfold emphasis on Scripture, tradition, experience, and reason can help us discern a Christian position on an issue.

Part of discerning a Christian position on a public policy issue is, of course, learning as much about the issue as you can. Many denominations have legislative newsletters you can request or e-mail groups you can join. Committees or Sunday school classes can work together to learn about public policy issues. National organizations like Bread for the World, a Christian citizens' movement on world hunger and poverty, send their members regular newsletters and legislative alerts.

> Scripture, tradition, experience, and reason can help us discern a Christian position on an issue.

Another part is determining whether this is a problem that can be dealt with most effectively by churches and faith communities directly or whether legislation needs to be part of the solution. If legislation should be at least part of the approach, is there legislation pending in your state or in the federal government? Have other states or localities addressed the problem with legislation? Is it most likely to happen at the local, state, or national level?

To find out the answers to these questions, you need the names and phone numbers of your state representative, state senator, United States representative, and your two United States senators. Most are happy to provide information to their constituents or at least to direct them to a website where they can obtain it.

As you evaluate politicians and policies, be humble and allow for the possibility of your own mistakes. Remember the words of Oliver Cromwell before the Battle of Dunbar: "I beseech ye in the bowels of Christ, think that ye may be mistaken."[11]

CHAPTER 9

A VISION OF CHRISTIAN CITIZENSHIP

Citizenship is the most important office.
U.S. SUPREME COURT JUSTICE LOUIS BRANDEIS

*Whatever makes a man [or woman] a good Christian also
makes a good citizen.*
DANIEL WEBSTER

*The first requisite of a good citizen in this Republic of ours
is that he shall be able and willing to pull his weight.*
THEODORE ROOSEVELT

For the believer, politics is one way among many to put faith into action. If you are a believer and a citizen of a free country, your faith will, whether you seek it or not, have a political expression. If you vote, hold office, or work for political and social causes, the many choices you make will reflect your conscious and unconscious conclusions about God and society. If you do not vote or otherwise engage in shaping your society, you are saying either that God has nothing to say about these matters or that you are refusing your own responsibility to act out your faith in this area.

Being a good citizen is hard work. It is also faithful work. It contributes to creating a society in which God's creatures can thrive and God's creation can be protected. It is good for you, for those you love, and for those who share life with you. Being a good citizen is an important responsibility, but what does it entail?

Indeed, the characteristics of a good citizen are many. Good citizens participate in the political life of society, showing respect for laws and the process through which laws are made. But they do not blindly obey laws that do not square with morality. As Dr. Martin Luther King, Jr. exemplified, good citizens support government when it is pursuing the right, and they courageously admonish and resist it when it is doing wrong.

Good citizens understand the important and relevant issues facing their community and do the difficult work of discernment to make informed decisions and to pursue their vision of good.

Good citizens express their opinions and have a voice in society, whether through their vote, letters to their representatives, involvement in a local community organization, or support of a political candidate. Good citizens also listen attentively and compassionately to the needs and perspectives of their fellow citizens.

Good citizens strive not only to prevent harm to their neighbors but also to actively advance the common good. They realize that their own well-being is tied directly to the well-being of others and that the ability of society and government to achieve justice, protect freedom, and save lives rests in their hands.

This vision of good citizenship does not seem very different from the vision of Christian citizenship, and frankly, it is not. Christians should share these same qualities—commitment, discernment, courage. But the Christian faith also calls Christian citizens to fulfill certain responsibilities that other good citizens may not have.

Christians are called to embrace others in the ways that Jesus embraced others—with respect, with humility, with compassion, and ultimately, with love. Following the example of Jesus—the one who was concerned not only about the law but primarily about love, justice, and liberation—is perhaps Christian citizens' greatest responsibility and opportunity. Above all, Christian citizens connect their vision of the good to God and strive to pursue God's will, always placing God before country.

CHRISTIAN PATRIOTISM

Christians can and should be patriotic, but Christian patriotism means, among other things, insisting that one's country live up to its own best values. When it does, we should be proud of our country; when it does not, we should admonish and seek to change it.

People of faith should attempt to shape our government institutions and laws in accordance with our understanding of God's will for the human family. But unlike other Americans, our final allegiance is not to our nation or to any other human institution. As the apostle Paul reminds us in Philippians 3:20, "our citizenship is in heaven," and our final allegiance is always to Jesus Christ.

> People of faith should attempt to shape our government institutions and laws in accordance with our understanding of God's will for the human family.

So for Christians, blind, unreflective patriotism is never an option. We are allowed only the eyes-wide-open, reflective kind of patriotism; the kind that acknowledges our God is the God of all the earth. The kind that never forgets that our brothers and sisters live and die all over this globe, not just within these United States. The kind of patriotism that knows that 360 million Christians live in Africa, 480 million in Latin America, and another 313 million in Asia.[1] The kind that sings "God Bless America, Land that I Love," but also sings the words of the 1934 hymn "This Is My Song":

> This is my song, O God of all the nations, a song of peace for lands afar and mine. This is my home, the country where my heart is; here are my hopes, my dreams, my holy shrine; But other hearts in other lands are beating with hopes and dreams as true and high as mine.

> My country's skies are bluer than the ocean, and sunlight beams on cloverleaf and pine; but other lands have sunlight too, and clover, and skies are everywhere as blue as mine. O hear my song, thou God of all the nations, a song of peace for their land and for mine.[2]

The best expression of Christian patriotism is being an active citizen in a free society working for *shalom*.

But how do we practically go about being faithful Christian citizens?

CHRISTIAN CITIZENSHIP

Citizenship, or membership, whether in a political system or in a church, requires more than just putting our names on the rolls but rarely or lukewarmly participating in activities. We are called to be citizens as we are called to be Christians—in word and deed. Citizenship is, as U.S. Supreme Court Justice Louis Brandeis taught, "the most important office."[3]

So how can we do justice to this most important office and still maintain our commitments to our family, our church, and our work? There is no way to know about every issue or every piece of legislation. Even legislators, with staff and lobbyists to help, have trouble keeping up with every bill.

> The best expression of Christian patriotism is being an active citizen in a free society working for *shalom*.

So, as in every part of your lives, you have to make choices. Choose one or two issues that you are interested in and have experience with, or even better, that tap into your deepest passions—issues that call for your faithful response and action. Examples might include abortion, welfare reform, capital punishment, criminal justice, world hunger, funding for AIDS research, school lunch and breakfast programs, government funding for stem cell or cloning research, or euthanasia and assisted suicide, just to name a few.

Once you have educated yourself about an issue and a piece of legislation, you should let your legislators know your position on the issue. On most of the issues that come before a legislative body, the elected representatives receive little from citizens. On a bill not dealing with sex or guns, I consider five letters or calls a groundswell of public sentiment.

Many citizens' groups recommend e-mail "blasts" to legislators, but a thoughtfully written personal letter is more likely to get the attention of your elected representative. If it is an issue you believe your elected representative needs educating about, make an appointment to sit down with him or her to discuss it. It is most helpful when my constituents come prepared and bring something in writing so I can go back over it later.

> Once you have educated yourself about an issue and a piece of legislation, you should let your legislators know your position on the issue.

Another way to become involved in the political process is to become active in a political campaign. Becoming active in a campaign does not necessarily mean you have to work as a full-time political operative. It may involve a one-time commitment passing out a candidate's literature at the polls on election day or helping with a get-out-the-vote effort by making telephone calls prior to the election. Or it may involve hosting a reception in your home to introduce a candidate to your friends. It could even involve something as simple as making a monetary contribution.

Whatever else one does to be a good citizen, there is one action that everyone must faithfully perform: voting! Every citizen, especially believers, ought not ignore the fundamental right that so many have sacrificed to win and protect.

And yet half of eligible voters fail to fulfill what President Lyndon B. Johnson called "the first duty of democracy."[4] If Christians seek to do justice, protect freedom, and save lives, they must vote. As a wise person once said, "The citizen who doesn't vote because he wants nothing to do with crooked politics, does have something to do with it."[5]

The motivation for political action and voting ought to be rooted in hope and love, not in hate and anger. We must be known more by what we are for than for what (or whom) we are against. As Jim Wallis says, "Hope has always been a more powerful force for change than despair. The renewal of our best values and moral sensibilities has the best chance of forging a new covenant."[6]

> The motivation for political action and voting ought to be rooted in hope and love, not in hate and anger.

Indeed, the quality of American government depends on the quality of citizens' political participation. "The greatest error of all in considering how to build an integral politics," Stephen Carter observes, "is to judge the integrity of our politics by the integrity of our politicians. In an electoral democracy, what matters far more is the integrity of the voters; in particular, what matters is the willingness of citizens first to envision a national purpose and then to vote consistently in ways that will further it."[7]

What is our national purpose? What is the Christian vision for America?

In truth, there is no single Christian vision because Christianity itself is diverse and not of one mind on all the issues. But there are common values and attitudes that all believers can embrace.

FAITHFUL VISION

Faithful politics needs a faithful vision. Wallis writes,

> When politics loses its vision, religion loses its faith, and culture loses its soul; life becomes confused, cheap, and endangered. Nothing less than a restoration of the shattered covenant will save us. That will require a fundamental transformation of our ways of thinking, feeling, and acting. At the core of prophetic religion is transformation—a change of heart, a revolution of the spirit, a conversion of the soul that issues forth in new personal and social behavior. ... We are suffering today not just from greed, injustice, and violence, but from a lack of imagination. For lack of a vision, we are perishing. We need new visions and dreams; our future depends upon fresh imagination.[8]

As Christian citizens, we are called to provide these "new visions and dreams" and this "fresh imagination" in politics. Wallis points out that the biblical prophets had two tasks: to tell the people the truth about God's righteousness and justice, and, in addition, to hold up an alternative vision to the status quo—that is, to show how things could be instead. Christians today need to perform both tasks in the political and social realm.

TRANSFORMING LEADERSHIP

Political scientist James MacGregor Burns contrasts transactional leadership with transforming leadership. Transactional leaders seek to exchange things. But transforming leadership "raises the level of human conduct and ethical aspirations of both leaders and led, and thus it has a transforming effect on both."[9]

Today we need transforming leadership, the kind implied in Paul's command that the believer be "transformed by the renewing of your minds, so that you may discern what is the will of God—what is good and acceptable and perfect" (Romans 12:2).

> We need Christian citizens and political leaders with eyes on the problems, not just the polls.

We need Christian citizens and political leaders with eyes on the problems, not just the polls; with ears for the possible, not just the popular. Thermostats, not thermometers. Winds of change, not weather vanes. Prophets, not profiteers.

We cannot make a difference unless we are willing to be different. As different as Jesus was and always will be.

If we would lead in transforming the world, then we must love.

Recall the words of Jesus when, as we saw earlier, he was asked which is the greatest commandment in the law:

> Thou shalt love the Lord thy God with all thy heart, and with all thy soul, and with all thy mind. This is the first and great commandment. And the second is like unto it, Thou shalt love thy neighbour as thyself.
>
> MATTHEW 22:37-39, KJV

Almost everyone recognizes that Jesus' command was to love. No word is more uttered, sung, declared, professed, and preached—but acted on less. We seem to think love is a noun, but it changes things only as a verb. Love is not simply good feelings we have for someone or something; love is God's grace in action.

Love is not a word used much in politics. Too few understand its power to transform societies as well as individuals. But our challenge as Christians is clear: to love our neighbors as ourselves. Only then will others know how Christians can be in politics. And only then will our politics be faithful.

ACKNOWLEDGMENTS

★

Writing a book with the word *Christian* in the title reminds me how far this sinner falls short. My family knows that best and yet both forgives and loves. My wife, Nancy, and our sons, John, Rick, and Ben, inspired and encouraged me while writing this book. John and Nancy also edited. I cannot thank all four of them enough for their help with the book and for so much more.

My mother is, and my late father was, a servant leader who never forgot the call to serve both God and neighbor. My late sister, Betsye, and brothers Ben and Dean always have been there for me in campaigns, public service, and other dubious undertakings. So have Nancy's parents, Fran and the late L.J. Miller, and her sister and brother-in-law, Jan and Dennis Dugan. I thank them all for their counsel, tolerance, and love.

I owe large debts to many Tennesseans, especially to the Seventy-sixth House District and Twenty-fourth Senatorial District. They have been my constituents and, in so many ways, my most faithful and patient teachers.

For over two decades, the members of the Tennessee General Assembly have been my teachers and mentors, colleagues and friends, prayer partners and fellow servants. I am grateful for their fellowship and faithfulness.

My indebtedness and gratitude extend to many other public servants working for the State of Tennessee and in national and local governments.

Mentors with whom I have been privileged to work include the late Congressman Ed Jones, Congressman Jim Cooper, Congressman John Tanner, Governor Ned McWherter, Governor Phil Bredesen, and Vice President Al Gore. Their leadership and integrity have influenced these pages and my own attempts to serve, and I am deeply grateful to each.

Many of the most faithful folks I know have been involved in politics. Stuart Brunson, Bob Cooper, Emmett Edwards, Bill Haltom, Johnny Hayes, Joe Hill, Mark Maddox, Gif Thornton, Byron Trauger and David Waters read or talked through ideas found here. They walk the talk.

Many ministers and church leaders have nurtured my faith and thus contributed to this book. In particular, Billy Vaughan and Greg Waldrop have helped me wrestle with religious vocation in the political world.

Scholars particularly influential in shaping this book and this writer include Matthew Black, John Donahue, Walter Harrelson, Larry McGehee, Ted Mosch, Tom Ogletree, Peggy Way, and Susan Ford Wiltshire.

Authors Will Campbell and John Egerton taught me to write, to trust God more than government, and to fight for progress.

For two decades I have learned from students at Vanderbilt University.

I especially thank the Divinity School classes Justice Ministry and Advocacy, Religion and Law, and Religion and Politics, and the Legislation Seminar classes at the Law School.

Stephanie Egnotovich edited my first book and nurtured ideas that became this one. I continue in her debt.

Josephine Binkley has been my legislative assistant for many years. I cannot say enough about the great job she has done for those we serve and for "grandmothering" our sons. Martha Stutts runs my law, business, and campaign offices. I am also greatly in her debt, particularly for her faithful witness and insistence that I do better.

Tyndale House in general and editors Mary Keeley and MaryLynn Layman in particular have been extraordinarily gracious, professional, and helpful. I know how much better a book this is because of their work, and you should, too.

The Vital Questions series editor Dan Taylor knew this book was in me, but neither of us anticipated his having to labor so hard for its birth. He is much more than an excellent series editor, and I am immensely grateful.

Michael Lamb has served as research assistant, editor, brain trust, campaign staff, running partner, and friend. He has also become like an older brother to our three boys and like a son to Nancy and me. Without Michael and Dan, this book truly would not be.

NOTES

INTRODUCTION

1. Anson Phelps Stokes, *Church and State in the United States* (New York: Harper, 1950), 1:512, quoted in A. James Reichley, *Religion in American Public Life* (Washington, D.C.: Brookings Institution, 1985), 104.

2. The Declaration of Independence, quoted in Pauline Maier, *American Scripture: Making the Declaration of Independence* (New York: Vintage Books, 1998), 148, 235-41.

3. Ibid., 148–49, 241.

4. James Madison, *Notes of Debates in the Federal Convention of 1787* (New York: Norton, 1987), 209–10, quoted in William J. Federer, comp., *America's God and Country: Encyclopedia of Quotations* (Coppell, Tex.: Fame, 1994), 150–51.

5. George Washington, "Farewell Address," September 19, 1796, quoted in James D. Richardson, *A Compilation of the Messages and Papers of the Presidents, 1789– 1897* (published by authority of Congress, 1899), 1:220, quoted in Federer, *America's God and Country*, 661.

CHAPTER 1 – HOW CAN A CHRISTIAN BE IN POLITICS?

1. J. Philip Wogaman, *Christian Perspectives on Politics* (Louisville: John Knox, 2000), 12–13.

2. *The Republic of Plato*, trans. Allan Bloom (New York: Basic Books, 1968), 100, 150; *Aristotle's Politics*, trans. Benjamin Jowett (New York: Random House, 1943), 52.

3. *The Republic of Plato*, trans. Benjamin Jowett, 4th ed. (Fair Lawn, N.J.: Oxford University Press, 1953), 32, quoted in M. Judd Harmon, *Political Thought from Plato to the Present* (New York: McGraw, 1964), 32.

CHAPTER 2 – WHAT DOES THE BIBLE SAY?

1. E. M. Good, "Peace in the OT," *The Interpreter's Dictionary of the Bible* (Nashville: Abingdon, 1962), 3:704.

2. Ibid.

3. C. L. Mitton, "Peace in the NT," *The Interpreter's Dictionary of the Bible: An Illustrated Encyclopedia* (Nashville: Abingdon, 1962), 3:706.

4. B. H. Throckmorton Jr., "Peacemaker," I*nterpreter's Dictionary of the Bible*, 3:706–7.

5. *The New Interpreter's Bible* (Nashville: Abingdon, 1995), 8:637. See also Bruce J. Malina and Richard L. Rohrbaugh, *A Social-Science Commentary on the Synoptic Gospels* (Philadelphia: Fortress, 1992), 238.

6. Ibid.

7. U.S. Census Bureau, *National Survey of Homeless Assistance Providers* (Washington, D.C.: U.S. Census Bureau, 1996), quoted in Martha R. Burt, "What Will It Take to End Homelessness?" October 1, 2001, Urban Institute, http://www.urban.org/url.cfm?ID=310305.

CHAPTER 3 – DOING JUSTICE

1. Proverbs 14:34: "Righteousness exalts a nation, but sin is a reproach to any people." Note also, shortly before this verse, Proverbs 14:31, "Those who oppress the poor insult their Maker, but those who are kind to the needy honor him," and Proverbs 14:32, "The wicked are overthrown by their evildoing, but the righteous find a refuge in their integrity."

2. For a particularly insightful discussion of biblical perspectives on justice, see John R. Donahue, "Biblical Perspectives on Justice," in *The Faith That Does Justice*, ed. John Haughey (New York: Paulist, 1977), 69–112.

3. Donahue, "Biblical Perspectives," 108.

4. Abraham Heschel, *The Prophets* (New York: Harper & Row, 1962), 16, quoted in Donahue, "Biblical Perspectives," 108.

5. Donahue, "Biblical Perspectives," 77.

6. Roland de Vaux, *Ancient Israel*, vol. 1 (New York: McGraw, 1965). Throughout this section, I rely upon de Vaux's excellent work, especially 68–76.

7. Ibid.

8. Samuel Driver, *Deuteronomy, International Critical Commentary* (New York: C. Scribner's, 1895), 267.

9. Ibid.

10. G. A. Barrois, "Debt," *Interpreter's Dictionary of the Bible*, 1:809.

11. Driver, *Deuteronomy*, 278.

12. H. H. Guthrie Jr. suggests that the most probable explanation of why tithes are not mentioned in the Book of the Covenant is that tithes and the offering of the first fruits are of common origin. (H. H. Guthrie Jr., "Tithe," *Interpreter's Dictionary of the Bible*, 4:654.)

13. Donahue, "Biblical Perspectives," 109.

CHAPTER 4 – PROTECTING LIFE

1. Arthur Kellerman, "Men, Women and Murder," *The Journal of Trauma* (July 17, 1992): 1–5.

2. U.S. Department of Justice, *Violence by Intimates: Analysis of Data on Crimes by Current or Former Spouses, Boyfriends, and Girlfriends* (March 1998).

3. Dr. Michael Decker, physician in preventive medicine at Vanderbilt Hospital in Nashville, quoted by the author in "Safe Babies or Highway Carnage," *The Tennessean*, March 6, 1989.

4. The hearings and this woman's testimony were in January 1989. According to the Tennessee Department of Safety, in 1987, 18

children under four died on Tennessee highways, 16 of them unprotected by safety seats. In 1988, another 18 children under four died on Tennessee highways and 15 of those were not protected.

5. Testimony of Dr. Allen Anderson, a pediatric surgeon at the University of Tennessee Hospital at Knoxville, citing a national study. His testimony was quoted in "Safe Babies or Highway Carnage."

CHAPTER 5 – DEFENDING FREEDOM

1. Walter Harrelson, *The Ten Commandments and Human Rights* (Philadelphia: Fortress, 1980), 20. Harrelson credits this view to Johann Jakob Stamm.

2. Ibid., 188.

3. This story comes from Karyn Henley, "Hard Times for Egypt," *The Beginner's Bible: Timeless Children's Stories* (Sisters, Ore.: Questar, 1989), 105–15.

CHAPTER 6 – CHARACTERISTICS OF FAITHFUL POLITICS

1. Colossians 3:12

2. Donald McNeil, Douglas A. Morris, and Henri J. M. Nouwen, *Compassion: A Reflection on the Christian Life* (New York: Doubleday, 1983), 4.

3. Ibid.

4. Ibid., 15.

5. Ibid., 17.

6. Ibid., 6.

7. 1 Corinthians 13:4

8. James 1:19

9. Christopher Matthews, *Hardball: How Politics Is Played, Told by One Who Knows the Game* (New York: Simon & Schuster, 1999), 132.

10. Ibid., 133.

11. Ibid., 134.

12. Colossians 3:12

13. Dwight D. Eisenhower, address at Guildhall, London, July 12, 1945, quoted in John Bartlett, *Bartlett's Familiar Quotations*, ed. Emily Morison Beck (Boston: Little, Brown, and Company, 1980), 815.

14. David Crockett, autobiography, 1834, quoted in Bartlett, *Bartlett's Familiar Quotations*, 455.

15. 1 Thessalonians 5:17

16. Jimmy Carter, *Living Faith* (New York: Random House, 1996), 104–5.

17. 1 Timothy 2:1-2, quoted in Carter, *Living Faith*, 97.

18. Luke 6:27

19. Ephesians 4:15

20. John F. Kennedy, *Profiles in Courage*, memorial ed. (New York: Harper & Row, 1964), 187.

21. Ibid.

22. Ibid.

23. John 16:33

24. Stephen L. Carter, *Integrity* (New York: Perseus Book Group, 1997), 7.

25. Andrew Jackson, quoted in Robert F. Kennedy, "Foreword to Memorial Edition," *Profiles in Courage*, ix.

26. Galatians 5:22

27. Carter, *Integrity*, 217.

28. G. K. Chesterton, *Orthodoxy*, quoted in Jim Wallis, *The Soul of Politics: A Practical and Prophetic Vision for Change* (New York: New Press, 1994), 233; also available online at http://www.chesterton.org.

29. Roy Herron and L. H. "Cotton" Ivy, *Tennessee Political Humor: Some of These Jokes You Voted For* (Knoxville: University of Tennessee Press, 2000), xii.

CHAPTER 7 – BEYOND PARTISANSHIP: SERVING GOD, NOT IDEOLOGY

1. Anne Lamott, *Bird by Bird: Some Instructions on Writing and Life* (New York: Anchor Books, 1995), 22.

2. Abraham Lincoln, quoted in Francis B. Carpenter, *Six Months at the White House with Abraham Lincoln* (New York: Hurd and Houghton, 1867), quoted in *Respectfully Quoted: A Dictionary of Quotations Requested from the Congressional Research Service* (Washington, D.C.: Library of Congress, 1989), Bartleby.com, http://www.bartleby.com/73/704/html.

3. Richard John Neuhaus, *The Naked Public Square: Religion and Democracy in America* (Grand Rapids, Mich.: Eerdmans, 1984), 114.

4. Carter, *Integrity*, 7.

5. Pope John Paul II, *The Gospel of Life* (New York: Times Books, 1995), 135, quoted in Carter, *Integrity*, 47.

6. Carter, *Integrity*, 47.

7. Kennedy, *Profiles in Courage,* 17.

8. Carter, *Integrity*, 46.

9. Leon Stein, quoted in Eugene E. Brussell, *Webster's New World Dictionary of Quotable Definitions*, 2nd ed. (New York: Prentice-Hall, 1988), 101.

10. H. L. Mencken, quoted in Brussell, *Quotable Definitions*, 441.

11. Abraham Lincoln, quoted in Brussell, *Quotable Definitions*, 441.

12. Walter Lippmann, quoted in Brussell, *Quotable Definitions*, 441.

13. Wallis, *Soul of Politics*, xix.

CHAPTER 8 – EVALUATING POLITICIANS AND POLICIES

1. Flannery O'Connor, *A Good Man Is Hard to Find and Other Stories* (New York: Harcourt Brace Jovanovich, 1977).

2. Stephen L. Carter, *God's Name in Vain: The Wrongs and Rights of Religion in Politics* (New York: Basic Books, 2000), 14.

3. Carter, *Integrity*, 52.

4. Much of this is taken from the League of Women Voters, "How to Judge a Candidate," *Smart Voter*, League of Women Voters of California Education Fund, http://www.smartvoter.org/voter/judgecan.html.

5. Ibid.

6. Ibid.

7. Ibid.

8. Ibid.

9. Braden Holton, legislative intern from the University of Tennessee at Martin, 2003.

10. Alan K. Waltz, "Wesleyan Quadrilateral, the," *A Dictionary for United Methodists* (Nashville: Abingdon, 1991), http://archives.umc.org/interior.asp?mid=258&GID=312&GMOD=VWD&GCAT=W.

11. Oliver Cromwell, letter to the General Assembly of the Church of Scotland, August 3, 1650, quoted in Bartlett, *Bartlett's Familiar Quotations*, 272.

CHAPTER 9 – A VISION OF CHRISTIAN CITIZENSHIP

1. Philip Jenkins, "The Next Christianity," *The Atlantic Monthly*, October 2002, http://www.theatlantic.com/issues/2002/10/jenkins.htm.

2. Lloyd Stone, "This Is My Song," *The United Methodist Hymnal* (Nashville: United Methodist Publishing House, 1989), 437.

3. Louis Brandeis, quoted in Brussell, *Quotable Definitions*, 86.

4. Lyndon B. Johnson, quoted in Brussell, *Quotable Definitions*, 593.

5. Evan Esar, *20,000 Quips and Quotes*, (New York: Barnes and Noble, 1995), 849.

6. Wallis, *Soul of Politics*, 149.

7. Carter, *Integrity*, 226.

8. Wallis, *Soul of Politics*, 41–42.

9. James MacGregor Burns, *Leadership* (New York: Harper & Row, 1978), 20.

TOPICAL INDEX

OTHER BOOKS BY ROY HERRON

★

THINGS HELD DEAR: SOUL STORIES FOR MY SONS

In the long tradition of Southern writers, Roy Herron vividly depicts the people, places, and circumstances that tie so many to the South. He paints a loving yet honest portrait of the region he calls home. These "soul stories" speak to all of us who nurture memories of our own people and things held dear.

TENNESSEE POLITICAL HUMOR: SOME OF THESE JOKES YOU VOTED FOR
(WITH L. H. IVY)

Ever since Davy Crockett's day, Volunteer State politicians have used humor to deflate their rivals, garner votes, and keep the public amused. Often the public has laughed at them—sometimes even when they were not telling jokes. This book offers a broad sampling of that wonderful comic lore, enriched over the years by Democrats and Republicans alike.

For more information, visit www.royherron.com.